AUTISM

AUTISM
A Practical Guide
for Parents and Professionals

MARIA J. PALUSZNY, M.D.

With Contributions from
JAMES L. PAUL, RONALD WIEGERINK,
REBECCA POSANTE-LORO, and MARIE BRISTOL

Foreword by
Eric Schopler

SYRACUSE UNIVERSITY PRESS
1979

Library of Congress Cataloging in Publication Data

Paluszny, Maria J
    Autism: a practical guide for parents & professionals.

    Bibliography: p.
    Includes index.
    1. Autism. I. Paul, James L., joint author.
II. Title.
RJ506.A9P27   618.9'28'982   78-31224
ISBN 0-8156-2212-0

Manufactured in the United States of America

To the families whose support and guidance made this book possible—

To my own family—Tony, Mark, Kiki, Taddy and my parents;

To my family of professional colleagues—
especially Drs. Cruickshank, Silverman, and Taren;

and

To the many families of autistic children who provided suggestions
and advice.

CONTENTS

Foreword   **ix**

Preface   **xiii**

1 The Autistic Child   **1**

2 Diagnosis   **21**

3 Etiology   **45**

4 Overview of Therapies   **69**

5 Educational Responsibility   **93**

6 Educational Programming   **115**

7 Parent Involvement   **131**

8 Future Planning   **149**

Bibliography   **159**

Index   **173**

CONTRIBUTORS

MARIA PALUSZNY, M.D., is Associate Professor of Psychiatry at the University of Michigan and Chief of Clinical Services and Assistant Director at the Institute for the Study of Mental Retardation and Related Disabilities. She has worked with children with emotional problems, developmental disabilities, retardation, and autism, and as a child guidance clinic consultant. She is currently Assistant Dean in charge of admissions at the University of Michigan Medical School.

MARIE M. BRISTOL, Ph.D., is a national program director at the Joseph P. Kennedy, Jr., Foundation in Washington, D.C., where she develops and implements training programs for families of handicapped children and for the professionals who work with them. She has developed parent-oriented comprehensive programs of services for preschool handicapped children and their families and was a fellow in the interdisciplinary Research Training Program at the Frank Porter Graham Child Development Center.

JAMES PAUL, Ed.D., has written extensively in the area of learning disabilities in children. He has worked as a teacher of emotionally disturbed children, as a consultant to the Department of Mental Health in North Carolina, and Director of Training in Developmental Disabilities at the Frank Porter Graham Child Development Research Center. Currently, he is Professor of Education and Chairman of the Division of Special Education at the School of Education, University of North Carolina, Chapel Hill.

REBECCA POSANTE-LORO, Ph.D., has worked extensively in the area of special education and has had experience as a research assistant. Clinically she has worked with both retarded adults and children and children with developmental and learning problems. She is currently employed by NTS Research Corporation conducting a national evaluation of the educational service components of Head Start.

RONALD WIEGERINK, Ph.D., is Director of the Developmental Disabilities Technical Assistance Systems and Project Director of Parent Involvement Studies in the Early Childhood Institute of the Frank Porter Graham Child Development Center. He was Chairman of the Division of Special Education at George Peabody College from 1970 to 1973 and is currently an Associate Professor of Education at the University of North Carolina at Chapel Hill.

FOREWORD

MORE THAN thirty-five years ago Leo Kanner first described eleven children who, with normal physical appearance, shared the bizarre behavioral characteristics Kanner called autistic. Similar children were identified in many other parts of the world as clinical and research activity concerned with this disorder grew over the years. Perhaps it was the children's aloofness that attracted attention, or Kanner's lucid description of their puzzling behavior, mysteriously suggestive of an underlying disease process. Whatever it was, the children received increasing attention from professionals of diverse backgrounds—psychiatrists, psychologists, teachers, social workers, neurologists, nurses, dentists, occupational therapists, musicians, physiologists, ethologists, psychometricians, psychoanalysts, biochemists, geneticists, speech pathologists, pharmacologists, dieticians, epidemiologists, psycholinguists, sociologists, and more. The children were relatively few in number, but their disabilities and the possible causes stimulated many areas of human interest and scientific inquiry which has resulted in flows of research—with cross-currents of diagnostic confusion, backwash of theory, and numerous branches of therapeutic and educational techniques.

Amidst complex research interests it is not easy to identify patterns of progress. It is a privilege to introduce a book in which the authors show the major changes of direction in the field at the level of practical application: the shift from viewing autism as a withdrawal from inadequate parenting to understanding it as a developmental disability; the change from regarding it as an intrapsychic, emotional disorder to be treated with individual psychotherapy to seeing it as a biologically based disability of childhood whose burden is shared among parents, school, and community. These trends have been presented with an eye to how they may practically affect those groups or professionals most frequently involved with this kind of child.

The first chapter is heavily illustrated by clinical experience, but it also emphasizes the developmental perspective needed by anyone concerned with autistic children. Like normal children, their behaviors, needs, and symptoms change with age. Even the child's most idiosyncratic symptoms are shaped, at least partly, by the child's age and level of development. The second chapter offers an admirably thorough discussion of diagnostic issues and how these impinge on different professionals. It leaves to the reader the challenge of understanding how the different professionals' diagnostic concerns may be integrated in understanding an individual child.

The third and fourth chapters most clearly reflect Dr. Paluszny's theoretical orientation: although no specific cause, or causes, for the autistic condition has yet been demonstrated, available evidence points to various biological impairments, each of which have the potential of contributing to the appearance of the syndrome. Various treatment methods are also summarized in the fourth chapter.

The fifth and sixth chapters are of special value for presenting the changing view of autism reflected in understanding the roles of parents and educators. In the fifth chapter these changes are discussed from the perspective of the administration and organization of professional services, with a concise summary of how they are directed through the political and legislative processes. In the sixth chapter these changes are traced through the educator's mission of programming special education for these children. In the seventh chapter the new and current understanding of the parents' role is presented, along with a discussion of how the parental role forms an integral link with the new directions in education.

New knowledge and progress continues even after the final words of these chapters have been written. Interestingly my Foreword to this book was written last, after the other chapters were completed. Even in the brief interval between Foreword and finished book manuscript, significant publications have appeared.

A companion volume offering more detailed research data to support the practical point of view detailed in the following pages is available [M. Rutter and E. Schopler, eds. *Autism: A Reappraisal of Concepts and Treatment* (1978)]. It includes Ritvo's critical review of biochemical and hematological studies, DeLong's analysis of temporal lobe irregularities, and Folstein and Rutter's twin study demonstrating a genetic link between autism and a broader range of cognitive disorders. The evidence for different etiological subgroups within the autistic syndrome is further documented in this volume. Equally important, it shows that the most effective educational strategies are not based on these underlying biological processes. Instead, the complex educational changes discussed by Dr.

Paluszny and her coauthors can best be implemented at present by individualized psychoeducational programming based on a developmental assessment of these children [E. Schopler and J. Reichler, *Individualized Assessment and Treatment for Autistic and Developmentally Disabled Children,* Vol. 1: *Psychoeducational Profile* (1978)].

Dr. Paluszny's book is meant as a practical guide that helps explain the controversies and confusion, a guide to the progress that has been achieved in our understanding and treatment of autistic children and their families during the past few decades. That the impressive progress in the understanding and treatment of autistic children is likely to continue in the future is heralded in the following chapters.

University of North Carolina
  at Chapel Hill
December 1978

ERIC SCHOPLER

PREFACE

Autism: A Practical Guide for Parents and Professionals presents a clinical orientation based on current theory and practice from the perspectives of many disciplines.

This book is designed not for the researcher or expert in the field of autism, but for the teacher, pediatrician, psychologist, psychiatrist, social worker, and speech therapist who work with autistic children or are interested in their problems. This book speaks to and for parents of autistic children who are often baffled by controversies in this field and may not understand how disagreements can arise and be resolved.

Autism presents problems in theoretical classification, diagnosis, etiology, and therapy. In almost every area there are different approaches, the most prominent of which have been summarized here and the most promising stressed. Since an interdisciplinary approach is necessary for such a complex problem, I sought advice and counsel from several disciplines in the writing of this book. Suggestions have been made throughout as to how existing community systems can be utilized to form interdisciplinary teams to work with the autistic child. Part of such a team are the child's parents, so this book includes information from a parent group.

Chapters 5, 6, and 7 present different aspects of the education of autistic children. A philosophical and historical perspective on the development of educational responsibility for these children focuses on the history of changes in educational philosophy and practices during the last fifteen years and gives primary attention to recent key federal legislation which mandates educational responsibility for autistic children.

The chapter on educational methodology describes psychoeducational and environmental approaches to teaching children with behavioral and perceptual disturbances which result primarily from the neuropathology of autism. The chapter on parents discusses the philosophies and practices of model parent therapy and training approaches.

Finally, the autistic child does grow up, and Chapter 8 addresses the issues involved in planning for the future.

Ann Arbor, Michigan   MARIA J. PALUSZNY, M.D.
Fall 1978

AUTISM

1

THE AUTISTIC CHILD

WHAT IS AUTISM?

Autism is a syndrome of childhood characterized by a lack of social relationship, a lack of communication abilities, persistent compulsive rituals, and resistance to change. A child with these characteristics does not relate to surrounding people, preferring instead to play repetitively with an object, a toy, or his or her own body. Language, if present, is severely impaired, but the child is aware of the environment to the extent that if the child's ritualistic play is interfered with, or even if familiar objects are changed in the environment, an upset or temper tantrum results. The syndrome's onset is usually in infancy—sometimes reported from birth, but certainly evident in the first three years of life.

Various names have been used to describe this syndrome: Kanner's syndrome, early infantile autism, early childhood autism, abnormal primary autism, encapsulated secondary autism, schizophrenia of the autistic type, atypical childhood development with autistic features, and mental retardation associated with autism.

Other terms have also been used, each aimed at clarifying a point around diagnosis or etiology. However, as the etiology is not known and some clinicians and researchers have conflicting opinions about this syndrome, much controversy has surrounded autism, both in diagnosing the condition and in uncovering a possible etiology. Furthermore, since autism is a rare condition, early studies were based on a few cases, and it was not until recently that large-scale studies and follow-up data appeared in the literature.

In this chapter, the historical development of defining autism will be considered. Autism will be described as it may become evident in a baby and child, and the incidence and prognosis will be discussed.

EARLY DEFINITIONS

In 1943, Leo Kanner reported eleven children who showed extreme with-drawal as early as the first year of life. He described various features of this syndrome, with the most significant feature being a lack of relating to people from infancy. Because of this self-imposed isolation, the syndrome was later named early infantile autism. In retrospect, researchers have found previously described cases of autistic or autistic-like children, but it was not until Kanner that the syndrome was identified as a diagnostic entity. The most famous of these early cases of probable autism, but not identified as such, is the case of Victor, the wild boy of Aveyron. In 1799, a boy about eleven years of age was found naked in the woods of Aveyron, France. He was dirty, covered with sores, mute, and behaved like a wild animal. Jean Itard, the physician of the new institution for deaf-mutes, was given charge of this abandoned child. From Itard's description, Victor showed many features of autism—he did not look at people and never played with toys, but showed a remarkable memory in recalling the position of objects in his room and resisted any change of these objects. Itard used positive reinforcement to educate the child, at first such simple reinforcers as a drink of fresh water. Even though therapy with Victor was not entirely successful, as he remained unusual in his behavior and never spoke, Victor did improve in that he eventually showed attachment to people and learned to communicate in nonverbal ways.

Researchers have found other examples of children described in the eighteenth and nineteenth centuries who were probably autistic, but as already mentioned, it was not until Leo Kanner described this syndrome that autism became a diagnostic category.

In describing early infantile autism Kanner mentioned, in addition to the extreme autistic aloneness, several other characteristics of the syndrome. These characteristics included an obsessive desire for the maintenance of sameness, lack of anticipatory posture in preparation for being picked up, lack of communicative speech, but often speech showing echolalia and parrot-like repetition. Kanner also found unusual special abilities in his group of children, such as good fine motor ability, an intelligent appearance, and extraordinary rote memory.

Following Kanner's initial description of the syndrome, other clinicians reported similar cases. However, as more studies were done, controversies developed. Questions about diagnostic criteria arose. Which symptoms were really the critical ones and which were sometimes associated with the syndrome, but not crucial in making the diagnosis? Was autism a separate entity or a variant of schizophrenia? Was it a variant of retardation? What about etiology? How much of the problem is psychological and how much physiological? Such unanswered questions, and attempts at prematurely answering them, occupied much of the early researchers' time. Since the 1960s, however, better research was conducted and progress has been more rapid.

There are still unanswered questions about autism, but some have been answered and others are partially answered. Even more important, various support systems for autistic children and their parents have been developed. Largely through the efforts of various pressure groups—such as parents of autistic children, developmental disability councils, and others—more facilities are available for autistic children. While day-care centers, mental health clinics, and public schools offer more and better services than previously, the services available are probably not nearly sufficient.

THE SYNDROME OF AUTISM

The term "autism" was first used by Blueler in 1919 to describe the withdrawal from the outside world seen in adult schizophrenics. Though this term as applied to the schizophrenic patient is quite different from the syndrome of autism, both have the similarity of an apparent preference for an inner world rather than external reality.

Autism, like many medical conditions first described as a syndrome, is defined and diagnosed by certain signs and symptoms rather than by specific etiology. This makes the problem of diagnosis complex. In illnesses where a causative agent can be found, the problem of diagnosis is relatively simple. For example, in a patient who has the symptoms of a prolonged cough and shortness of breath (and the objective signs show persistent fever and density of the lungs on chest x-ray, and laboratory findings disclose pneumococcal bacteria in the sputum), the diagnosis is pneumonia. No one will quibble as to when the symptoms first were noted, or if the cough is dry or sputum-producing, or if rales could be heard in auscultation of the chest. These are minor points which may be useful in steering the physician to do a sputum culture and chest x-ray, but once the diagnosis is made, minor differences in the way the patient demonstrates the illness are unimportant.

Unfortunately there is no specific test for autism; rather, autism is defined by its symptoms. As different clinicians and researchers have stressed different symptoms as the critical ones, discrepancies in the diagnosis of autism are frequent. We shall consider the diagnosis of autism from an interdisciplinary perspective, but at this point, typical symptoms will be discussed as one may see them develop in a child who shows autism versus a child who does not have this illness.

SYMPTOMS

Pregnancy

Generally, the pregnancy of the mother of an autistic child is no different from any other pregnancy. In some cases, maternal bleeding during pregnancy has been reported, in others prematurity of the infant was present, but neither of these problems has been found on a consistent basis. The incidence of maternal rubella (German measles), however, has been related to autism. In one study (Chess 1971) children who had congenital rubella showed a higher incidence of autism than that found in the general population.

Infancy

Frequently, parents of the autistic child note no problems in the first or second year of the child's life. The baby appeared normal in all respects. In retrospect, the parents describe an exceptionally attractive baby who showed an initial period of happy responsive behavior. Later, generally sometime before the third year, a regression occurred. The child lost his previously acquired skills, and some of the typical symptoms of autism were noted.

With many autistic children, however, parents note a difference in their baby almost from birth. The parents cannot pinpoint exactly what the difference was but they describe a vague feeling that something was wrong from infancy. Frequently, this difference from other babies is a form of social unresponsiveness.

In usual child development, one of the first milestones is the social smile. Babies usually smile in response to an adult face or voice at one month of age; certainly by two months this response is expected. An autistic child may appear happy and contented, but his smile is not a social smile; it occurs as a response to sights, sounds, and other stimuli but not in response to the caretaking adult.

The normal baby readily reacts to the mother's face. The baby smiles and explores the face by looking at it, touching it, and poking fingers into mother's eyes, mouth, and nose. The autistic child rarely looks at mother, characteristically showing no eye contact and failing to explore her features. Likewise, the child does not react by crying when the mother leaves or by laughing when she approaches. Most babies by eight months of age show stranger anxiety. Prior to that time, most babies will smile at anyone; but at six–eight months most babies regard strangers with apprehension, and often cry if a stranger tries to pick them up. The autistic baby does not seem to differentiate between strangers and familiar people. He appears disinterested in people in general, and does not respond either with pleasure to family or with signs of stress to strangers.

Likewise, an autistic infant does not show play behavior with people. He does not show anticipatory posture in being picked up, nor does he engage in the games frequently seen in normal infants. Games like "peek-a-boo" or "pat-a-cake," which most one-year-old babies play readily, are of no interest to the autistic child. He may enjoy sensory-stimulatory games such as tickling, being tossed in the air, or riding "horsie" on someone's shoulder, but none of these games requires interpersonal interaction.

Parents of autistic children frequently report how "good" the baby was as an infant. This is because such infants prefer to play alone. Often the infant may be preoccupied with a sight (a light) or a sound; or, he may create his own sights and sounds by spending hours watching a flicky finger in front of his face, or scratching on the bedsheet. He may be completely absorbed by stimulating his own body, by rocking, or by head-banging. This self-stimulatory or stereotypic fondling of objects becomes even more noticeable later. However, even in infancy, parents note that their autistic child shows little curiosity—he does not explore his environment, preferring instead to play with objects repetitively or to stimulate his own body.

The second important milestone in the psychosocial development of the baby is vocalization. This usually occurs in the second month of age and by three months most babies will utter sounds. At first these sounds can be just squeals and coos, but by six months the baby will use these sounds to "talk" to toys and persons. By seven or eight months, such sounds will usually be definite consonants—"ma-ma," "da-da"—and by ten months these sounds will refer to the specific person. By one year of age the average baby can gesture when he wants something. He will say two additional words (as well as Momma and Dadda), and the parents will note that the baby can understand much more. For example, "give me" or "wave bye-bye" can be understood and demonstrated. The autistic baby does not show this social development. He does not show appropriate language, nor does he communicate by imitation or gesture. The problem of speech in the autistic child is a central one. The child seems unable to understand or respond to language. This problem, however, may not be noticed in the autistic child until much later. The baby may learn one or two words and use them repeatedly in an indiscriminate fashion. The parents and pediatrician, seeing language but not recognizing that it is used inappropriately, may not be concerned about this aspect of language development until the child is three or four years old.

By contrast to the lack of psychosocial development, the motor milestones of most autistic infants are usually on schedule. There may be a delay in some of the motor milestones, but usually the delay is slight. For example, most babies sit by seven or eight months of age and begin walking at twelve months. The autistic child may sit at nine months and begin walking at fourteen or fifteen months. Occasionally, autistic children may show early development, such as walking by nine or ten months. However, the motor development is not entirely normal as the child may show unusual movement such as walking on tiptoes, spinning, or showing unusual posture while standing still. Again, however, as the child is just learning to walk, peculiarities of motor development are often disregarded as immaturities which the child will overcome with time.

In summary, even in infancy many autistic children show variations in development. This is most prominent in the psychosocial development, but slight variations may be seen even in motor development. Frequently, however, these differences are ascribed to immaturity, and it is not until much later that the pediatrician and others become concerned.

Early Childhood

As the autistic child begins his second and third year, pre-existing difficulties are heightened and new problems emerge. The lack of social relationships becomes more and more obvious. Most toddlers actively follow mother around, imitating her and exploring their environment. The autistic child does not seem to be aware of the persons in his environment. He is most content if left alone to play repetitively with some toy or object. He may spend hours spinning or rolling a toy. The play is stereotypical, repetitive, and shows no variation; the toy is used in an idiosyncratic manner unrelated to its actual function. If this play is interfered with, the child may show a terrible temper tantrum.

Repetitive body movements such as rocking or head-banging, which were seen in infancy, become more prominent and draw the parents' attention to the child's apparent lack of reaction to pain. The child may show a lack of response to other stimuli, coupled with an oversensitivity to still other stimuli. For example, the child may ignore a loud noise but appear fascinated or even fearful of sounds such as rustling of paper or the sound of food frying. Many autistic children seem especially fascinated by spinning objects. Likewise, spinning or twirling their own bodies has a special attraction, and may be repeated together with hand flapping and rocking whenever the child is excited. Sometimes such excitation, just like the temper tantrums, seems unprovoked. The child laughs or screams without apparent reason. Occasionally the child cries, but many parents of autistic children say that crying with tears is something they rarely see.

Toilet training is often very much a problem with autistic children. Through various encouragements most children are toilet trained with more or less difficulty by the age of three years. Autistic children, however, show much resistance to toilet training. Some may be toilet trained early but may show persistence of fecal smearing or similar behaviors long after they are trained.

By two years, most children establish regular eating patterns. The autistic child may show peculiarities in the type or quantity of foods he eats. He may avoid certain common foods, e.g., milk, but consume either sporadically or routinely large amounts of other foods. For example, one autistic boy had a history of refusing milk since infancy. When he was admitted to a psychiatric facility he continued this refusal, and also showed wide variations in his appetite. For days he ate almost nothing, then in one meal he could eat more than two adults. The child had no nutritional deficiencies and at six years of age his height and weight remained average, despite his peculiar eating habits. At this time, he routinely ate a small to moderate lunch and dinner, but for breakfast ate up to ten eggs each day!

Communication—especially through continuous, improved language proficiency—is very noticeable in most two-year-old children. By two years, average children begin to use pronouns such as mine, me, you. Between two and three years of age, average children use "yes" and "no" routinely, can refer to themselves by name, can name several common objects in picture books, and begin to show mastery of abstract concepts through language. The abstract concepts are simple but significant in the child's continued understanding of himself and his environment. For example, most children by three years will say if they are a boy or a girl and can accurately identify other pictures of boys and girls. They begin to use prepositions, can name colors, and are learning to count. Most important, if all else fails, the two- and three-year-old child can gesture if communication by verbal skills is insufficient by showing his parent what it is he wants.

Autistic children characteristically show problems in language development. Speech may be present but it is not used for communication. Pronouns, if used at all, are usually reversed. For example, to the question "Do you want a drink?" the autistic child will respond "You want a drink," typically not using the pronoun "I." "No" is sometimes used by these children, but "yes" is used very rarely or not at all. Echolalia or repetition of what an adult says is a frequent response.

These problems with language involve the entire area of communication. The autistic child typically does not mimic, gesture, use posture, use intonation, or attempt to convey meaning by any other mode of verbal or body language. The normal two-year-old child will grab a glass if he wants a drink, or he may lead his mother to the refrigerator or sink. The autistic two-year-old child is more likely to climb onto the sink or to scream, giving his mother no clue as to what it is he wants. Even if some gestures are present, these are not communicative; the autistic child may wave "bye-bye," but the action is not related to someone leaving. Often the autistic toddler may scream incessantly (apparently wanting something), then stop abruptly, leaving his parents totally confused as to what it was he wanted.

Later Childhood and School Age

By the time an autistic child is three or four years of age, his family physician and even friends and relatives are concerned about the child's unusual development. Problem areas first noted in infancy or early childhood become more obvious as the child continues to show a deviant path of development from his peer group.

By four years, most children show increasing independence and socialization. They can dress themselves; feed themselves; communicate their wants and wishes verbally; and play with other children, not just in parallel fashion, but by cooperating and taking turns. In contrast, the autistic child frequently shows unusual behaviors in feeding and dressing, continues to act as a social isolate, and prefers to play alone.

Rituals and stereotypical behaviors may be present in dressing and undressing. Likewise, small changes in the child's environment or daily routine can set off tantrums or periods of severe anxiety. It is as if this child remembers minute details, and any changes in these details can precipitate a calamity. This is illustrated by Fred, an autistic boy of four. Fred enjoyed his weekly visits to the university speech clinic. Because Fred reacted to even minor changes in the drive to and from the clinic, his mother always took the same route and never stopped for errands on the way. One day Fred had what appeared to be a totally unprovoked tantrum in the car. He screamed, banged his head, and seemed completely out of control. In reviewing the details of the drive, the mother finally realized that in order to pass a slow-moving vehicle, she changed traffic lanes, and this altered the route she usually travelled. This minor change was sufficient to cause Fred's upset. Other parents report that minor changes in the autistic child's room or toy arrangements cause similar temper outbursts.

Fascination with repetitive stereotypical play continues to be the major preoccupation of these children. Some autistic youngsters develop a strong attachment to a particular toy or object. The real intent or function of the toy or object is immaterial. Peter, a five-year-old autistic boy, carried a telephone book with him much as a younger child would carry a security blanket. At the age of three or four he spent hours flipping the pages in the book. He never turned the pages one by one, but always flipped them in a fan-like manner. By the time he was five his parents and therapist managed to get Peter to perform other activities, but he still carried his telephone book everywhere he went.

Verbal communication continues to be a major problem as these children grow. Language ability in the three- and four-year-old autistic child may be completely lacking—an absence of comprehension and no expressive language ability. Frequently some language development is seen, but it is disturbed. The autistic child may show delayed echolalia; he will repeat long monologues (such as TV commercials), but he cannot use speech to communicate. Normal children will also frequently memorize TV commercials, but their memorization is different in that they often substitute a word or paraphrase portions of the speech, thus indicating they understand some of the material they are repeating. The autistic child does not substitute words; he repeats verbatim. The tone and intonation of the verbal production also varies in normal and autistic children. The normal child, in repeating something, usually mimics and imitates the tone. The autistic child usually has his own speech pattern and will not use intonation.

Some autistic children use limited verbal production for communication, but here again, distortions are present in the form of pronoun reversal, repetition of questions, or a repetition of their own remarks (echoing). Even if some speech is present, there is no abstract comprehension of language. Some of these unusual patterns will change later as the autistic child develops, but frequently speech idiosyncrasies persist. For example, Peter (the autistic boy who carried the telephone book with him) eventually developed speech. By the age of eight years he could communicate quite well, but his speech showed no intonation or punctuation; he spoke so rapidly that words ran into each other. He learned to communicate by writing, but he wrote just like he spoke. One day Peter wrote an observation about his teacher: "Stanhasabigsiga" [Stan has a big cigar].

With older autistic children, an area of frequent concern to parents and therapists is the violent, often unprovoked temper tantrums and aggressive attacks. Even though temper tantrums are present in younger autistic children, they seem less dangerous both because of the child's small size and his relative limitations in mobility. As the autistic child grows, he has both the opportunity and ability to seriously hurt himself and others. A three-, four- or five-year-old can pound his head on the wall or the floor much harder than a one- or two-year old child. An older child can also strike out and hurt younger children or even adults. Furthermore, this striking out at others occurs in many autistic children. Even though the older autistic child still relates to those around him in only a marginal way, he is relatively more likely to strike out and hurt persons in his environment than is the younger autistic child.

Steve, an autistic child treated in an inpatient psychiatric facility, illustrates this point. At the time of admission, Steve was 5 years old. He was a withdrawn, nonverbal child who demonstrated anger and anxiety in a ritualistic, stereotypical manner. When upset, Steve blew his nasal contents onto his hands and smeared his face, neck, and hair with these secretions. (Remarkably, he always could produce secretions even though he rarely had colds and had no allergies.) As therapy progressed, Steve began to smear not only himself but the ward staff. When the staff learned to control this behavior, and could stop Steve before he smeared them, Steve showed a new aggressive tactic. Initially, these aggressive acts were random and consisted of hitting, biting, and scratching, but within a year Steve began to use scratching primarily. The scratching seemed unprovoked. Steve appeared content or preoccupied with an activity; then he would suddenly lash out at a staff member and scratch the latter around the eyes. His speed was so great and his accuracy so precise that a number of the staff had corneal lacerations from Steve's attacks; at one time the problem was so pervasive that at any staff meeting one could identify the people working with Steve by the scratch marks on their faces! The behavior was gradually eliminated by negative reinforcement of scratching and positive reinforcement of gentle behavior. Steve was isolated if he scratched. In addition, his favorite staff member spent time each day with Steve, allowing Steve to touch and explore his face— especially his eyes. This staff member had particularly good rapport with

Steve, was never frightened of the child, and despite the exploratory sessions was never scratched. (This technique, though, cannot be recommended as a routine behavior modification method!)

As described above, the unpredictability, speed, and ability of the older autistic child to produce real damage can be frightening to the child's parents and therapists.

Another area of interest (and, at times, frustration) in the development of the autistic child are the special abilities these children occasionally demonstrate. For example, even though many autistic children show a delay in motor or psychosocial development, it is not unusual to find premature spurts in development of these areas. Some autistic children may actually be early in walking, while others—though not early—may suddenly begin walking with such skill and balance that one wonders if they did not have this ability earlier. Although the autistic child typically shows speech retardation, he may learn several new words within a period of a few hours. Memory for minutiae and detail is often seen in the autistic child. Not only does he remember details in his environment and his routine, but in addition he may recall such things as page numbers from books. For example, Peter often spoke to himself in a rapid, screechy manner. Once, when he clearly articulated the name "Alexander the Great," his therapist asked where he obtained the information; Peter responded by quoting the page number in the encyclopedia where he read this passage.

Clinicians working with autistic children have frequently reported unusual rote memory for poems, names, and even spatial relationships. Some autistic children are particularly skilled in arranging jigsaw puzzles, doing such tasks even with the picture turned face-down.

Musical ability with perfect pitch is sometimes found in autistic children. In rare instances, even remarkable musical ability—leading to the child's becoming a musician—has been reported.

CASE EXAMPLE OF AN AUTISTIC CHILD

Peter was initially evaluated when he was three years old. Although the primary reason for the evaluation was Peter's lack of speech development, the parents were also concerned about Peter's other unusual behaviors. Particularly they were concerned that Peter preferred to be alone and he never looked directly at his parents.

At that time, Peter was an only child. A younger brother was born when Peter was four years old. According to the background information, both Peter's parents came from middle-class intact families in which no significant psychiatric or medical problems were present. Peter was a wanted child, and the pregnancy was uneventful. However, the labor was difficult, lasting fourteen hours, and according to calculations Peter was one week post-mature. He weighed seven pounds eight ounces at birth, and there were no problems in the initial neonatal period.

Peter was described as a quiet baby who did not cry much. His early development was normal, in fact, somewhat earlier than average; i.e., Peter sat up at five to six months and began walking at nine months. He was toilet trained at two years, but persisted in having daytime and night-time accidents. Frequently at such times Peter would be very upset, having a temper tantrum, but would never come to his parents for help. At other times Peter would also have temper tantrums; these usually occurred when his routine was changed or when his play was interrupted. For example, Peter spent long hours arranging one block in front of the other. The parents referred to this as Peter's "train." The "train" had to remain in the same position until Peter decided to take it apart; otherwise, a temper tantrum resulted.

Usually Peter was content to play by himself, but if he was taken to a new setting he would cry, and at such times he clung to his mother. His parents felt Peter was not affectionate, but it was not till the lag in language development became obvious that they became truly concerned. Peter did learn a few words; he could say, *mama, dada,* and *car.* But his usage of the words was not always appropriate and usually unpredictable. For example, one day Peter would use these words but then for weeks say no words at all. He could then learn a new word, say it repeatedly for a day, but then *never* use that same word again. Thus, *mama, dada,* and *car* were the only three words he spoke at the time of evaluation.

His parents also noted Peter had a peculiar response to sound. He would react with fear to certain sounds, especially any motors such as the vacuum cleaner, refrigerator, or lawn mower. Sometimes he seemed hypersensitive to these sounds, reacting by crying if he heard one of these sounds even at a low volume. At other times, he did not react to loud noises or even to the noises that he seemed to be fearful of. In particular, he frequently ignored speech. His parents complained that Peter often "tuned them out."

In the evaluation, Peter reacted angrily at being separated from his mother. He clung to her and screamed. However, when they both came into the office, Peter left his mother and played with a toy car. He did not explore the office and the toys, nor was he interested in the examiner. During the evaluation he performed certain tasks, such as building a tower, completing an eight-piece puzzle, and drinking from a cup. He did not show right or left hand preference, but had no problems in gross or fine motor coordination. Occasionally, he made screaming noises while playing. He could follow some gestures, that is, by demonstration he started to match colors, but he could not complete the task and it was uncertain how much of the matching was accidental. During the evaluation he never approached his mother or showed eye contact with her or the examiner.

From this evaluation it was felt Peter was probably an autistic child. Other evaluations were done, including a physical, neurological, an EEG, and an audiological exam. These evaluations showed no abnormalities, except the EEG—which was mildly abnormal though not specific—and the audiological, which showed fluctuations of responses, though no discernible hearing impairment was found.

Initially, therapy for Peter consisted of weekly visits to an outpatient child guidance clinic and speech therapist, and in addition enrollment in a private nursery school. His mother was seen at the guidance clinic on a weekly basis, and the therapist and mother shared suggestions of what seemed to be working in getting Peter to relate to people and his environment. In addition, frequent meetings were held between the guidance clinic, speech therapist, and the nursery school teachers. The parents attended all of those meetings.

In therapy at the guidance clinic, Peter's therapist initially attempted to involve herself in Peter's play. Peter typically came to the office and began arranging his toy "train" from blocks. At first, he did not react when the therapist handed him blocks, nor did he react when she spoke to him. Gradually he began to accept the blocks from her, but still showed no eye contact or other response. One day, however, Peter indicated he was aware of his therapist. At the end of every session, Peter's therapist gave him a piece of candy from a drawer in her desk. Peter always took the candy and left. On this particular day, Peter left his play with the "train" earlier, took the therapist's hand, and gestured toward the drawer where the candy was located. Following this episode, Peter had many more periods of unresponsiveness; but with the cooperation of home, nursery school, and guidance clinic therapist, he began to use gesture much more frequently in communication.

Over the next three years, Peter continued to make progress at nursery school. He began to explore play materials and became especially interested in books. He was first fascinated by flipping pages, and this in fact had been an activity that Peter was fond of even as a toddler. Typically he flipped the pages of the telephone book, but finally gave up this activity and just carried the telephone book around with him. One day, with no prior warning, Peter demonstrated that he could read and write. While waiting in the guidance clinic, Peter explored the secretary's typewriter and began to type words. The words all ran into each other but, nonetheless, they could be easily identified as the names of various states. Peter later used the telephone book as a way of communication. He could find the listing of his parents' name, his therapist, and other people he knew. His speech, however, lagged behind these areas. Although Peter began putting sounds together during the second year of therapy, his speech was very difficult to understand because of pitch, articulation, and an inability to separate words. Spontaneous speech was rare, even though Peter could repeat long paragraphs.

Peter remained in the nursery school four years. By that time, the school had a kindergarten class and was able to individualize the program, so Peter was taught skills at a higher level. He was never a behavior problem at school, and in fact showed much fear and avoidance of any child who was aggressive. Apart from this avoidance, he rarely interacted with other children. He did, however, interact more with adults, and continued to show much progress in academic skills. In fact, reading was his favorite activity.

When Peter was eight years old, a new day treatment unit was opened by the clinic. Peter was placed with several autistic and emotionally disturbed children. The emphasis in this setting for Peter was on development of verbal skills and peer interaction. Meanwhile, Peter continued to see his therapist, who by this time was an important person to Peter. Peter remained in the day treatment unit four years. During that time, Peter showed more peer interaction, began using pronouns correctly, and continued to improve in other areas. However, outside of the school setting Peter tended to stay to himself and was reluctant to get involved with children in the neighborhood.

When Peter left the day treatment unit it was initially planned to integrate him into public school, but since there were concerns about adequate programming for Peter in the school, he was finally enrolled in a boarding school which accepts both retarded and emotionally disturbed children. In addition to Peter, there were several autistic youngsters.

At this time, Peter is sixteen years old. He is a handsome boy who is functioning at school in most areas at the 9–10 grade level. He comes home during holidays and enjoys being home, but is also happy when he has to return to his school. Recently, he visited the clinic and met with his therapist and a consultant he had also known for many years. Peter stated he recognized both of them, but affectively he showed little response. He still avoids eye contact and verbal interaction. When questions are asked, Peter responds in phrases using the least number of words possible.

Theoretically, one can assume Peter will progress at the same rate; he can probably adjust to a work situation and can probably develop independent living skills. However, his social adjustment will probably remain marginal.

In reviewing Peter's case, several points should be made. Peter was evaluated and treated at a time when autism was still viewed as a disorder primarily related to an unhealthy environment. Despite this prevalent attitude, Peter's therapist and several consultants involved in the case questioned the possibility of an organic impairment, especially since Peter's parents seemed particularly responsive to the child's needs. For this reason, a consistent effort was made to provide Peter with a proper schooling environment, and therapy in the traditional sense was only ancillary. Peter had access to several educational systems geared toward children who have learning problems; he always attended special schools and was never enrolled in a general school program. Likewise his therapist used educational techniques such as gesture rather than formal psychotherapy aimed at discovering underlying conflicts and unacceptable strivings.

Another factor acting in Peter's behalf was the relative mildness of his disturbance. Although in many ways Peter represented the classic autistic child—his lack of relating, stereotypic behavior, lack of language development—he still showed two positive factors. First, on several psychological evaluations Peter showed an average IQ (ranging from 90 to 102). Secondly, Peter was never an aggressive or oppositional child. In fact, aggression was quite fearful to Peter. Whenever he observed children fighting, Peter cowered. Once, when a disturbed child hit him, Peter became so anxious he had to remain home from school for several days and avoided that child thereafter. Many of the aggressive problems prevalent in autistic children were never an issue with Peter. Despite all these positive points, Peter still has not "recovered." At this time, he is functioning well in many areas, but his social interactions still leave much to be desired.

PROGNOSIS

Several long-range follow-up studies have now been done on autistic children. In these areas, as in other studies of autistic children, there is the ever-present confusion of terminology. But even with this difficulty, certain trends can be seen. The prognosis for most autistic children is poor. In Kanner's follow-up study, only a small percentage of autistic children were integrated into society. Of a total of ninety-six autistic children seen by Kanner prior to 1953, only eleven were reported to be doing well. These eleven were employed, all owned cars, and most were generally independent (only three of the eleven continued to live with their families). They had some social activities through hobbies and clubs, but none were married; nor had they even seriously considered marriage. Generally, dating or intimacy was avoided by this group. Even the successful autistic children had persistent problems in the area of social adaptation.

The less successful autistic children fare much worse. Many show few independent skills and little or no language development, and a high proportion are institutionalized. In a follow-up study of sixty-three autistic children, Rutter *et al.* (1967) found almost half of the group showed a poor adjustment and were not capable of independent living. About a quarter of the group had made some gains in social adjustment and were showing independence to some degree. Only one-eighth of the group, however, was functioning well despite some personal oddities. Only one child was functioning at a completely normal level. Thus, the hope expressed by many parents and professionals that the autistic child will show a complete recovery seems most unlikely. In fact, if by six or seven years of age an autistic child does not show good progress, the likelihood of good progress being made past that age is slim. It is important to note that most of these early follow-up studies were done on children who had little, if any, special schooling. As this is an important factor, it is possible these early follow-up studies are overly pessimistic regarding prognosis.

Another aspect of follow-up studies has been an attempt to identify which factors lead to a more successful outcome; that is, what interventions would improve the child's prognosis and what symptoms, if present (or absent), would be more indicative of a less successful outcome. Some factors were identified as being useful indicators of outcome while others did not appear to influence the prognosis. Earlier studies on autistic children indicated that the child's language ability prior to the age of five was a good indication of eventual outcome. Recent studies partially confirm this finding, that the age five is not particularly significant but language ability acquired at whatever age is very important. In fact language ability and IQ are the two most important prognostic indicators. In the past when IQ testing of autistic children was frequently not done the best measure for eventual outcome was language. With better assessments of the autistic child's intelligence now being done it is apparent that the child's IQ on initial testing also correlates with a better prognosis. The *best* prognosis is for those children who showed an IQ near normal and minimal language impairment. Where the child's IQ was judged to be below 50 on the initial testing and there was no language development, the prognosis was the poorest.

Two other items that influence outcome are the overall severity of the syndrome and the amount of schooling. If the total severity of all the symptoms was lesser, the prognosis was better. If the autistic child received more schooling and education, the prognosis was also better. In one study—which also confirmed the above findings—parental warmth, consistency, and adequacy of communication did *not* seem to influence the outcome. Also, the type of therapy used with the child did not seem to influence the outcome (Rutter 1974).

Another interesting finding on follow-up studies was the high incidence of epilepsy found in autistic children. By the time these autistic children reached adulthood, almost ¼ of them had seizures (Rutter 1970). This finding, as will be discussed under etiology, suggests an organic impairment. Before discussing potential and/or possible causes, we should consider the incidence and pattern of autism.

EPIDEMIOLOGY

Since autism is a rare syndrome, initial studies were done on only a few cases. With time, as more and more clinicians and researchers studied larger samples of autistic children, epidemiological data became available. In the past ten years, large samples were drawn from normal children and clinic patients in order to determine the incidence of autism and other related data (Treffert 1970; Lotter 1966; Rutter 1967; Wing 1976).

Three such large-scale studies, sorting hundreds of children to assess how many showed autism, were conducted in the U.S. (Wisconsin), in England, and in Denmark. Though there were some variations in the results, the differences could be explained on the basis of difference in the samples and methods of study. These studies confirmed that autism is a rare condition, with the prevalence varying from 0.7 to 4.5/10,000 in the different studies. Generally, it is estimated the incidence of autism is 3–4/10,000.

These major studies also considered variables such as sex ratio, order of birth, and socioeconomic status of the parents. Earlier studies indicated a much higher incidence of autism in male children, as did these studies. The lowest ratio of male to females was in the Denmark study where there were 1.4 male autistic children for every 1 female. In the

British study (in the group that was considered "nuclear," the group that was most clearly autistic according to symptoms), the ratio was 2.75 males to 1 female. The Wisconsin study showed the highest male to female ratio—3.4:1.

A word of caution should be inserted at this point regarding the male to female ratio. This higher incidence in males should not give voice to speculations about etiology. It is well known that most disorders, whether physical, mental, or emotional, affect the male child more frequently than the female. For example, in children with minimal brain dysfunction (also called learning disabled or hyperkinetic), the ratio of males to females has been estimated to be anywhere from 25:1 to 15:1 (Cruickshank 1977). It is generally accepted that the male infant is more delicate and vulnerable to illness and injury. Furthermore, the usually larger size of the male infant may make the baby more susceptible to injury during the birth process.

The order of birth of the autistic child has been assessed in the three studies mentioned and in other earlier studies. Some of these earlier studies showed a higher incidence of the problem in first-born males. This finding, however, has not been substantiated in the recent large-scale studies. In these, there was no clear pattern in the birth order of autistic children.

The socioeconomic status of the parents of autistic children has been a topic of controversy. In his initial description of infantile autism, Kanner found a very high incidence of autism in children of highly educated parents in the upper socioeconomic group. In a later study (Kanner and Lesser 1958), he found that almost 90 percent of the occupations of the parents of autistic children would qualify as the upper social class (social class being defined by the parent's occupation and education). Other investigators, however, found different results. In one study, comparing 74 autistic hospitalized children with 74 non-autistic children hospitalized for other psychotic problems, the investigators found no significant difference in the socioeconomic status of the parents of the two groups of children (Ritvo et al. 1971). Most investigators, however, did find a higher incidence of autism in the children of parents in the upper socioeconomic group, but nowhere near as high as reported by Kanner. Thus, despite controversy in this area, it appears that autism does occur somewhat more frequently in families of the upper socioeconomic class.

Related to this issue is another observation Kanner initially made of the parents of autistic children—namely, a high incidence of an intellectual, aloof, efficient, but cold type of parent. Earlier investigators confirmed this finding, which was linked to etiology. However, subsequent studies have not shown a characteristic personality type. Nor was evidence found that there were greater environmental stresses, or a particular type of family interaction, in the homes of autistic children.

In overview, autism appears to be an illness present frequently from infancy and certainly having its onset before three years of age. The syndrome consists of a variety of signs and symptoms, particularly characterized by a lack of social interaction and withdrawal, an abnormality in language development, and the presence of ritualistic compulsive behaviors. The prognosis is generally poor, with IQ and language ability being the most useful predictors of adult adjustment. It is a rare syndrome, occurring in 3–4 children per 10,000. No definite birth order has been established; autism does occur about three times more frequently in boys than in girls, and it occurs somewhat more frequently in the upper socioeconomic group.

2

DIAGNOSIS

From the preceding chapter it may appear that the symptoms of autism are unique, so diagnosis should be relatively simple. Actually this is not true. Separating autism from other conditions is often difficult. There are problems in several areas. First from a theoretical standpoint the question has arisen whether autism is a specific entity or if it is a form of schizophrenia or of mental retardation. Secondly, from a practical standpoint it is difficult to assess if a child is autistic or if he is suffering from another disturbance.

In this chapter we shall consider the criteria of diagnosing autism from a theoretical perspective and discuss some thoughts concerning the classification of autism. Finally we shall present a practical model of the function of an interdisciplinary team in diagnosing and prescribing for an autistic child.

CRITERIA USED TO DIAGNOSE AUTISM

Kanner's initial description of eleven autistic children presented a comprehensive picture of the syndrome. In fact, the critical symptoms he described have not changed significantly since that time. Here were Kanner's major points.

1. The child showed inability to relate to people and extreme autistic aloneness.

2. The child failed to assume an anticipatory posture in preparation to being picked up.

3. There were speech problems; some were mute; others showed delayed echolalia; personal pronouns were repeated just as heard; there was literalness in comprehension of speech.

4. The child had an anxious obsessive desire for the maintenance of sameness.

5. There was limitation in the variety of spontaneous activity.

6. The child reacted to external intrusions such as food, loud noises, and moving objects.

7. The child was interested in objects and reacted to people as part objects—when pricked, the child showed fear of the pin but not of the person who pricked him.

8. The child had excellent rote memory.

9. The child was physically normal, showing good cognitive potential and serious-mindedness.

10. All autistic children come from highly intelligent families.

Following Kanner's description, other investigators discovered similar children. However, soon it appeared that autism was becoming fashionable and was being over-diagnosed. In an effort to refine criteria various investigators and groups set down critical points and developed rating scales for disturbances such as childhood schizophrenia and autism. Polan and Spencer (1959) developed a checklist that addressed five categories: (1) language distortion, (2) social withdrawal, (3) lack of integration in activities, (4) obsessiveness and nervousness, and (5) family history.

In 1961 a group (The British Working Party) under the direction of Mildred Creak (1964) formulated a nine-point diagnostic checklist as a guideline for diagnosing childhood schizophrenia. These nine points describe autistic children but the criteria refer to schizophrenic and include other groups as well as autistic children. Rimland (1964, 1974) developed a diagnostic questionnaire that could be filled out by parents. This checklist is aimed at differentiating autistic children from other groups including schizophrenic children. Lotter (1966) designed a checklist when he studied the incidence of autism in Middlesex, England. DeMyer and Churchill (1971a) diagnosed autism on the basis of Kanner's major points—(1) emotional withdrawal before the age of three, (2) lack of speech for communication, (3) nonfunctional repetitive use of objects, (4) failure to engage in role play alone or with other children. The autistic child was differentiated from the child with early childhood schizophrenia in that the schizophrenic group showed (1) islands of more normal relatedness and (2) some speech for communication, with speech abnormalities.

Rating scales cause problems. In discussing such approaches Kanner (1969) stated, "the children have not read those books." Variations occur and a child cannot fit a diagnostic template. Furthermore, in comparing these various schemes for diagnosing autism, one can readily see there are areas of overlap but there are also many differences. DeMyer (1971b) compared some of these rating scales, comparing Rimland's scale, DeMyer and Churchill's system, Polan and Spencer's checklist, Lotter's checklist, and the British Working Party's classification. They found there were many areas of overlap in the various systems. Despite this, a group of children received high scores in one system and were diagnosed as autistic, while the same children, when diagnosed according to another system, received low scores and were rated as not autistic.

Rutter (1974) pointed out it was necessary to define which of the many symptoms of autism were found in *all* autistic children and were significantly less frequent in other diagnostic groups. When this was done, only three symptoms were found to be essential to the diagnosis and also specific to this group of children. These three symptoms were:

1. Profound and general failure to develop social relationships.
2. Language retardation with impaired comprehension, echolalia, and pronominal reversal.
3. Ritualistic or compulsive phenomena.

Rutter found four other symptoms which were more frequent in the autistic group but were not found in all autistic children. These four were: (1) stereotypic repetitive movements, (2) a short attention span, (3) self-injury, and (4) delayed bowel control. Rutter's three specific symptoms generally confirmed Kanner's observations, and these critical symptoms are the key criteria used by most workers to diagnose autism.

One area in Kanner's original description merits further discussion. Kanner initially felt that autistic children had normal intellectual potential. In fact, because of remarkable rote memory, autistic children were thought possibly to have a high IQ. The lack of responsiveness was felt to be the reason why cognitive skills could not be adequately assessed. As more investigations were carried out in the area of intellectual ability it became clear that autistic children function at all levels of intelligence. In fact, most autistic children show an IQ in the retarded range.

Whether an autistic child is retarded or not has certain implications in terms of prognosis (retarded autistic children have a poorer prognosis). Retarded autistic children show greater behavior problems of more self-abuse, delayed social development, greater perceptual difficulties and more neurological problems such as seizures. The non-retarded group have more problems in other areas—pronominal reversal, peculiar sensitivities to sound and rituals. Generally however the similarities between the groups outweigh the dissimilarities (Bartak and Rutter 1976).

Differences in IQ and the severity of symptoms of autistic children make it mandatory to carefully assess the specific areas of skills and areas of impairment for each child. Before considering the area of practical diagnosis, however, another area related to the theoretical aspects of diagnosis needs to be considered, namely the classification of autism.

THE CLASSIFICATION OF AUTISM

Early investigators of autism considered this syndrome as a subgroup of schizophrenia. The severe problem in relating, the use of speech in an inappropriate and idiosyncratic way, and the general impression that these children had good cognitive potential seemed to differentiate the autistic syndrome from other psychiatric disturbances and from retardation. It appeared more reasonable to change the previous attitude that a normal period of adjustment must precede the development of schizophrenia and, as Kanner (1949) suggested, view early infantile autism "as the earliest possible manifestation of schizophrenia." Later, as more studies on autistic children appeared and a large number of autistic children were found to function in the retarded range, the question arose as to whether or not autism should be grouped with retardation. Various authors have addressed these questions from a number of perspectives, but unresolved issues remain.

Those investigators who believe autism is a separate entity point out several differences between these disturbances. The incidence of schizophrenia in childhood shows highest concentration in two age groups. The first highest concentration occurs prior to two and a half years of age and the second peaks in adolescence. The first peak may represent infantile autism and the second the onset of schizophrenia. Thus the time of onset is different and there is no continuity between the onset of the two syndromes. Secondly, autism shows a uniform course, not marked by the remissions and relapses characteristic of schizophrenia. The hallucinations and delusions typical of schizophrenia are not typical—in fact, are very rare—in autism (Rutter 1974). Some demographic differences are found in autism and schizophrenia. Parents of autistic children rarely have schizophrenia, but there is a 10 percent incidence of the illness in parents of schizophrenics. The sex ratio is different, with autism being more common in boys (4:1) while schizophrenia shows an equal male/female ratio. Finally, mental retardation is frequently associated with autism but not with schizophrenia. In reviewing these and other differences Miller (1974) points out that there are other syndromes with early onset, and thus the syndrome described as early infantile autism by some workers may not be one entity but actually several. Schizophrenia may include several different entities with autism being one of these. Thus the controversy over the classification of autism as an early onset of schizophrenia or as a separate entity continues.

This controversy is not critical in conceptualizing autism. Whether or not autism is an early form or sub-group of schizophrenia sheds little light on the condition of autism, as schizophrenia itself is largely an unknown entity.

A similar controversy has arisen in separating autism from mental retardation. Since autistic children frequently have low IQs and since retarded children often show peculiarities of behavior, should autism be considered a type of retardation? Here the answers are somewhat easier. First, not all autistic children are retarded. Second, the degree of retardation cannot explain the child's autism as there are *more* retarded children who are not autistic. Thus, autism may be present in conjunction with retardation but is not a result of or a type of retardation.

How can autism be categorized diagnostically? Currently, autism is classified in two different ways. In most psychiatric or mental health clinics, autism is classified under psychotic disorders of childhood. From what we now know about autism, this is an acceptable classification. Psychosis does not imply etiology—it may occur as a result of an organic impairment or as a functional disorder. Psychosis simply describes mental functioning which is sufficiently impaired in adaptation and perception of reality to interfere grossly with a person's capacity to meet everyday life. Thus autism is a form of psychosis. Another way in which autism may be classified is as a developmental disability. Recent work in the area of etiology of autism has produced evidence of an organic impairment. Today most researchers believe a central nervous system defect causes sufficient cognitive deficits to prevent the autistic child from learning to relate normally to his environment. Thus his impairments are a type of developmental disability. Recently many groups of children are being called developmentally disabled, and it has been suggested that more groups be included—childhood schizophrenics, those with learning disabilities. The term soon could become so general as to be meaningless.

Possibly the most reasonable way to classify autism is to use a "multi-axial" approach. This has been proposed by the World Health Organization and combines a descriptive with a functional classification. Basically the system involves four axes. "The first specifies the clinical syndrome; the second the intellectual level; the third any associated or etiological biological factors; and the fourth any associated or etiological psychosocial factors" (Rutter 1972). This system is useful in classifying any child psychiatric disturbance, but would be especially useful in a syndrome like autism where there has been much confusion and controversy in each of these four dimensions.

Unfortunately, this system is used rarely. Instead autism is usually simply placed in a category and decisions are made on the basis of this assigned label. Such practice can be particularly important in the autistic child's school placement. Mandatory special education laws provide for the development of a program for each handicapped child in many states. Often, however, the way a child is "classified" rather than individual needs can determine the type of program. In an educational placement and planning committee (EPPC) meeting it is quite likely that the same autistic child could be placed in different programs depending upon how his diagnosis is classified. If autism is called "psychotic," a classroom for emotionally disturbed children will probably be recommended, whereas if autism is called a developmental disability, a different setting may be recommended. Thus it is exceedingly important not only to diagnose an autistic child accurately but to include clarification of the child's special needs for programming. Educating an EPPC meeting on the problems of classification can be useful. One of the ways such educating can be done is by involving the school personnel in the actual process of diagnosing and planning. In the next section we shall discuss a format for involving school personnel in an evaluation as well as a description of assessing an autistic child from an interdisciplinary perspective.

INTERDISCIPLINARY DIAGNOSIS OF AUTISM

Because the autistic child has problems in a number of areas it is useful to utilize several disciplines to formulate the diagnosis and to assess the child's level of functioning. The model described here is routinely used at The Institute for the Study of Mental Retardation and Related Disabilities (ISMRRD) for evaluation of all children, to determine whether the child has learning disabilities, retardation, autism, or even only a neurotic problem. The disciplines are selected on the basis of the suspected diagnosis (or differential diagnosis) and history obtained from the child's family and previous clinical records. In evaluating a child suspected of being autistic, the following disciplines are usually employed: audiology, pediatrics, psychiatry, psychology, special education, speech and language, and social work. Neurology is usually not involved unless the pediatrician feels a neurological evaluation is warranted. If fine or gross motor areas need to be assessed, physical therapists or occupational therapists may be included in the evaluating team.

Prior to the actual evaluation the team members meet to discuss strategies and areas to be assessed. At times two disciplines may want to do a joint evaluation. For example, special education and psychology often elect to work together.

After the strategies are mapped out the evaluations are scheduled, usually over a two- or three-day period. All the evaluations are done on an out-patient basis, but arrangement can be made for the family to stay at a local hotel if the family lives far from the clinic.

Many of the evaluations of an autistic child are conducted in a room with a one-way mirror. The parent together with a staff member, while observing the evaluation process, can discuss procedures and ask questions, and the parents can discuss how they think the child would handle the same task at home. Some disciplines often use the parents to administer portions of tests. This is frequently done by special education and psychology, who can use these observations of parent-child interaction in formulating their recommendations.

After the evaluation process is completed and all the reports are written, the staff meet to discuss their findings and recommendations. During this staff meeting all the information is pulled together to formulate a diagnosis, to discuss differences of opinion, and to decide on specific immediate as well as long-range goals. The team leader (who is designated on a rotational basis) is then responsible for pulling the information into a summary document which includes evaluations by individual staff members as well as final recommendations. The team leader meets with the parents and discusses this composite report.

The second meeting or "interpretive" session includes members of the evaluation team, the parents, and appropriate community resources such as school personnel, guidance clinic personnel. During this interpretive meeting, findings are discussed and decisions are made as to which recommendations will be used and how they can be implemented. Usually the parents and community agencies are responsible for carrying out the details of the recommendations, but the clinic staff remains available as consultants whenever this is necessary—if problems arise or as additional sources of information for an EPPC.

To give some sense of an interdisciplinary evaluation, several clinicians from the Institute for the Study of Mental Retardation and Related Disabilities were asked to describe how they evaluate an autistic child. From the following descriptions, the different approaches can be seen as well as different goals and objectives in the evaluations. Some of these clinicians focus primarily on differentiating autism from other conditions such as congenital deafness, language delays, or retardation, while others emphasize the delineation of the child's impairments and skills and still others focus more on prescription for future planning.

It should be noted that in evaluating an autistic child, special education is always involved. Since this area is discussed in detail in Chapters 5 and 6, an evaluation approach from special education has not been included in this chapter. Approaches from audiology, social work, speech and language, pediatrics, psychology, and psychiatry are included here.

Audiology*

The autistic child may be evaluated by an audiologist either as part of a multidisciplinary assessment or as a referral from a pediatrician who wants to rule out a hearing loss as a possible cause for the child's lack of responsiveness. Frequently children who are congenitally deaf appear unresponsive, show speech delay, and may easily be confused with an autistic or retarded child. Even if a child is known to be autistic, a peripheral hearing loss could be present in addition to the child's autism. For this reason an audiological assessment is important in differential diagnosis and in assessing the possibility of a partial hearing loss.

The deaf or hard-of-hearing child exhibits many characteristic behaviors which are familiar to the experienced observer. Typically the child with a severe hearing impairment is acutely in touch with his environment both visually and tactually. He is sensitive to subtle visual changes and he reacts quckly to touch or to vibration. He tries very hard to communicate by gestures or by facial expressions, and he seeks eye contact with others. He is lively and alert, active and exploratory. His response inadequacies occur only in the auditory dimension. If he becomes withdrawn, it is secondary and occurs only after a long period of frustration with his inability to communicate his needs. This behavioral repertoire is in sharp contrast to the generalized lack of responsiveness, withdrawal, and impaired relationships seen in the autistic child. Differentiating deafness from autism on the basis of observation is not difficult. What is more complex is the identification of milder degrees of hearing impairment in the child who is autistic.

Although there is no evidence that the incidence of peripheral hearing losses among autistic children is any higher than among a population of normal children, it is not always easy to recognize the presence or absence of a true hearing loss in these children because their general response behavior is functionally so atypical. Traditional methods of testing hearing are seldom successful with the autistic child. When testing a child's hearing the audiologist generally relies on the child to cooperate and to respond voluntarily to various tones and other sounds on the basis of verbal directions ("raise your hand when you hear the sound") or within the context of a game. This is the way that hearing tests have been

*The Audiology section was written by Elizabeth Soper, M.A., Program Associate in Audiology, ISMRRD.

standardized and is the only truly valid way to compare an individual's hearing thresholds with normal. It is unlikely that the autistic child, given his behavioral symptomatology, will be so cooperative as to allow this kind of testing. How then can the audiologist contribute to the diagnostic or intervention team working with the autistic child?

There are ways by which an audiologist can assess, with fairly good accuracy and validity, the adequacy of a child's hearing despite the typical unwillingness of the autistic child to respond to standardized tests. Specialized procedures and equipment for eliciting responses to sounds have been developed for other groups of people who are difficult to test, and they can be successfully applied to autistic children. These include the measurement of involuntary, reflexive reactions to sounds and behavior modification procedures designed to minimize the need for interaction between the examiner and the test subject.

Most people, even autistic children, will react when unusual sounds are presented. Similarly, almost all people (assuming they hear normally) will exhibit an uncontrollable "startle" reaction in the presence of a sudden loud noise. Techniques involving the pairing of an attractive visual object (for example, a lighted toy or dancing monkey or moving cartoon) with a sound have been successfully used to "condition" difficult-to-test children to look toward the visual reinforcer when they hear a sound. This procedure is called Conditioned Orienting Reflex Audiometry (or CORA). Another technique uses a machine that dispenses edible reinforcement (candy or sweetened cereal) when the child pushes a button in response to a sound. This procedure is referred to as Tangible Reinforcement Operant Conditioning Audiometry (or TROCA).

There are also "objective" hearing tests which can measure the functioning of the ears and hearing mechanism without the need for any voluntary response on the part of the subject. Changes in brain wave patterns, heart rate, respiration, skin resistance, and electrical potential within the inner ear itself occur automatically in the presence of sound, and techniques have been developed to measure all of these phenomena under controlled stimulus conditions.

In the process of hearing assessment the audiologist's observational skills again can be uniquely utilized. The audiologist is trained to be aware of and alert to subtle changes in behavior that can indicate that a child hears even in the absence of more overt responses. The audiologist also is sensitive to carefully controlling the test environment so that extraneous stimulation does not interfere with the auditory signals used for testing.

In working with the autistic child, either at the stage of diagnosis or in treatment, it is essential to know whether his hearing is intact or whether it may, in fact, be impaired. The audiologist as a member of the diagnostic/intervention team can contribute to the total pool of knowledge about the child by assessing and describing this essential sensory modality. The information so obtained will influence the approaches used in treatment of the child and additionally will allow for the remediation of secondary problems that may be imposed if a hearing loss does exist.

Social Work*

A social worker is able to contribute to the diagnostic and treatment process provided to the family of an autistic child in a variety of ways. Members of an interdisciplinary team rely on the social worker to present information about the dynamics present in the family, with special attention to the patterns of interaction among the various family members, as well as the individual family member's perception of the autistic child and his or her place in the family. A social worker should be prepared to provide the interdisciplinary team with a description of the routines within the family home and the procedures the family has established for maintaining these routines. It is important for the team to have an understanding as to the unique limits and rules for behavior that are important to the child's family, and an awareness of how these limits and rules are introduced, modeled, enforced, and rewarded. An interdisciplinary team needs to have information about how the parenting responsibilities are shared in the child's family with special attention given to identifying how behavior is managed in benign as well as crisis situations.

Once a treatment process has been determined, efforts must be made to help parents handle their feelings so that they may mobilize their energies to help their child. It is important to recognize that the bonding between parent and child is based on a never-ending chain of responses between parent and child. The very condition of autism results in the disruption of this chain of responses, and the parent ends up giving, giving, giving to the child without the encouragement of the child's responses. Simply stated, the more a child gives pleasing responses, the more loving attention will the parent provide. This mutually satisfying process is notably absent in the relationship of parent and autistic child. The parent needs to hear from the social worker that it *is* difficult to love the child who does not respond and even rejects or rebuffs the parent's attention.

As the parent is given recognition and support around the difficul-

*The Social Work section was written by Martha U. Dickerson, M.S.W., Program Associate in Social Work, ISMRRD.

ties of loving a "non-loving" child, specific strategies and interventions
are introduced to the parent so that a positive impact may be made upon
the child's growth and development. Parents must be helped to accept
the idea that loving alone will not accomplish a positive impact upon the
child, but rather their loving must become active and intrusive.

Parents need to gain understanding that their child may not be a
good candidate for remediation, but that the child may be able to achieve
a level of performance more socially acceptable. Parents should be
taught how to develop and maintain a highly structured family and home
environment in order for the child to develop skills in self-care and social
interaction.

In order to introduce new or preferred behaviors parents must be
helped to learn that they must make demands upon the child, they must
insist that the child pay attention, and they must establish or re-establish
control in every interaction. The social worker should discuss with the
parents the reasons behind such adamant interventions and provide modeling, role-playing, monitoring, and support while the parents learn the
techniques. Parents must be encouraged to play and talk with the child
even when there is no response.

The social worker can provide instruction and modeling as to ways
of managing bizarre or difficult behaviors, including tantrums. Parents
should learn to ignore odd movements and grimaces and introduce di-
verting activities. The social worker can help parents modify the environment and the parenting style in order to prevent unacceptable behavior.
The designation of a room or play area where the child's messy play is
permitted will make it easier for the child to accept other areas of the
home which are not used without supervision. The social worker can help
the parent develop skills to handle tantrums and destructive behavior. As
the parents learn to become intrusive, demanding, insistent, and actively
loving parents, their feelings of inadequacy and guilt will lessen. Parental
confidence and security will develop as they learn to set limits, to determine priorities, to recognize the cues given by the child, and to provide
consistent, constant, assertive affection. Parents will develop comfort
and skill in relating to professionals about their child as they gain as-
suredness in their skills at home. In the best of situations, parents may
become central figures in an interdisciplinary team providing opportunities to the child, in contrast to the situations where parents appear to be
"also there." Here again the social worker can be useful as a liaison between home and school, eventually leading both parties to interact more
openly with each other.

Some parents may wish to gain insight into their own behaviors, attitudes, and perceptions, so that they may have a greater understanding of themselves as parenting people. Insight development should be encouraged and the social worker can be an enabling person in this process.

The social worker on an interdisciplinary team working with an autistic child should provide interventions which will serve to stabilize the home environment, enhance parenting skills, and strengthen the relationship between the home and the community resources.

Speech and Language*

The role of the speech pathologist in the diagnosis and treatment of the autistic child is a primary one. The parents of this puzzling child frequently begin their search for diagnostic answers at a speech and hearing clinic, since the child is unresponsive to speech and has either no language or unusual patterns of communication.

Expressive and receptive language skills are only two of the windows into the child's world. Any evaluation by a speech and language pathologist may include an evaluation of movement and behavior, cognitive skills and inner language, expressive language varying from mutism to deviant language patterns to distorted communication strategies, and receptive language. The techniques for evaluation will depend on the child's abilities, age, and experience. For instance a nonverbal child who relates poorly to pictures and objects will be assessed in a different way than will the child who is capable of more formal testing.

Let us look more closely at four areas of communicative abilities: (1) behavior, (2) learning, (3) expressive language, and (4) receptive language.

BEHAVIOR

An evaluative setting is difficult for many children; they are separated from parents, are asked to do new and often difficult tasks, and they are unsure of what is expected of them. The autistic child who often cannot tolerate stimulation, who is anxious and upset, who is dedicated to maintaining an undisturbed equilibrium, and who has difficulty establishing relationships with people is certainly at a disadvantage. He may resort to bizarre or ritual-like behaviors, obsessions for sameness and resistance to any environmental change. His nonverbal behavior, such as gestures and body language, should be observed.

*The Speech and Language section was written by Carolyn Eckstein, M.S., Program Associate in Speech and Language Pathology, ISMRRD.

LEARNING

Before a child learns to talk and understand language he must have an inner language or something to talk about. The acquisition of inner language involves two processes: the ability to acquire concepts and the ability to code these into language and symbol systems for efficient recall. An autistic child frequently shows difficulty learning new skills from his world.

A good way to evaluate these behaviors is to observe free toy play. The child's play appears inappropriate to the intended function of the specific toy. The child may throw or pound the toy, regardless of what it is. The child does not use the toy to play out symbolic or make-believe situations (such as talking on a toy telephone), but may use it only in a motor way, like spinning the receiver of a telephone. In general, the child's toy play appears to be manipulative, not symbolic. In play as at other times, he will not interact with the examiner.

EXPRESSIVE LANGUAGE

Mutism

From 25 to 50 percent of the autistic population is mute. Other autistic children show verbal communication which varies from a few noises to jargon-like utterances. The autistic child sees little need for interpersonal contact, and his verbalizations often represent a type of energy release through the vocal mechanism that are really devoid of communicative intent. In fact, quite frequently the vocalizations are described as "autoerotic" rather than "interpersonal." The noises the child may employ are guttural and self-stimulatory, unlike linguistic phonemes found in usual language. The overall production is usually devoid of any normal-sounding words, even though it may be quite animated or enthusiastic. Often this jargon-language may be accompanied by musical or rhythmic intonation.

Deviant Language Patterns

Whether or not the child can speak in words and phrases is a very important prognostic indicator of his future adjustment. Most autistic children show a marked delay in language usage, and even those who use words and phrases often show deviant language patterns. These unusual language patterns of the autistic child are summarized in Table 1.

AUTISM

TABLE 1

Deviant Language Patterns Described in Autistic Children

Kanner	pronomial reversals, echolalia, "irrelevancies" due to personal metaphor.
Pronovost	rote repetition
Cunningham & Dixon	egocentric speech, incomplete sentences, incomprehensible responses
Boucher	repetitive, stereotyped responses; echolalia; recitations of rote learned sequences; meaning of a phrase may be highly idiosyncratic
Vetter	immediate or delayed echolalia; absence of spontaneous sentence formation

It is generally felt that the forms of the autistic child's linguistic interactions reflect the way the child associates with his world. He is unable to relate to past communicative experiences or draw efficiently and automatically on a linguistic code. He is rarely able to formulate a question spontaneously or display the inner language he has acquired. This is seen in his tendency to repeat exactly what is said to him rather than constructing an appropriate response. Consequently the child demonstrates pronoun reversals, "you and your" frequently being used instead of "I, me, or my" and affirmative or negative phrases are used rather than directly answering "yes" or "no" to a question. Much of his response pattern is echolalic (either immediate or delayed), limited, and stereotyped, and the linguistic form used may not be matched to the stimuli. These metaphorical substitutions give his language a quality of inappropriateness. Often the autistic child will recite a stereotyped utterance where semantically the word-meanings do not match the context. One may need to explore the child's past experience in order to determine the true meaning of the child's response. For example, "Don't throw the dog off the balcony" actually meant "Don't do that" to one child. Another child responded, "Johnny Smith is a good boy" whenever he was asked his name; or, another child said, "It's the Pepsi generation" when asked if he wanted a drink of soda. This failure to abstract an appropriate code from what is heard and a tendency for specific stimuli to trigger highly specific verbal responses are examples of what has been called the "concreteness" of the content of autistic language.

Apart from expressing basic needs appropriately the use of the autistic child's language is limited in scope and variety and appears idiosyncratic. He has a personalized communication system, replete with neologisms (made-up words) and familiar words used with idiosyncratic meanings. His system of communication does not appear to be acquired through natural interaction, imitation, and parent stimulation of speech and language. The speech and language history of these children often show limited pleasurable sound play, infrequent vocal imitation, and a lack of imitation of facial and other gestures.

Autistic language differs from other severe language disorders. A disorder which affects communication and can possibly be confused with autism is childhood aphasia. However, autistic children do not have many of the errors in speech and language seen in severe aphasia. Very few developmental delays in articulation proficiency are noted in the autistic population. In addition, autistic children generally show no discrepancies between single word and sentence comprehension. In aphasic children sentence comprehension is much poorer. Autistic children usually associate sound and meaning accurately; for example, the rustle of paper is associated with sweets. They also have normally developed sound localization skills and are able to sequence sounds in words and words in sentences. Aphasic children usually do not have such skills.

Distorted Communication Strategies

In addition to noting the unusual format of autistic communication, it is important to determine the abnormal language strategies the autistic child uses in his speech. The suprasegmental features of language—those features of speaking which carry meaning and "color" our words, such as rate, inflection, and vocal tone—are often deviant. The autistic child's voice is monotonous, oddly pitched, and inclined to wander. It can be described as an abnormal delivery system in communicating with his world.

The autistic child's communication is severely impaired in still another regard. His nonverbal communication is not supportive of what he is vocalizing. In usual interpersonal communication, nonverbal skills or body language are very important carriers of information. Autistic children often have a complete absence of nonverbal communicative intent. They employ no facial gestures, maintain inappropriate posture or stance, do not use eye contact constructively, and their movements are bizarre or unrelated to the verbal message delivered. This is quite different from hearing impaired children who rely heavily on use of visual contact, gestures, mimes, or facial expression as a mode of communication. The interactional quality of the autistic child's language is distorted in voice quality, unusual suprasegmental features, and incongruent or absent nonverbal communication systems.

RECEPTIVE LANGUAGE

The autistic child is frequently described as demonstrating "self-absorbed inaccessibility" and unusual response to speech and stimuli in his environment. He may show abnormal attending to auditory, visual, olfactory, gustatory or vestibular sensations (as shown by ear banging, staring, sniffing, or excitation with spinning objects). A heightened sensitivity to the same stimuli may be seen (fearful reaction to noise or ease of distraction by noise, strong reaction to changes in illumination).

There are many stages of attending to speech and language or receptive speech and language development. The autistic child's growth pattern in receptivity to language must cover a wider excursion as he begins with obliviousness and withdrawal from the significant and crucial stimuli. Normal children are perceptually set to process much information from their environment. Their neural centers are very "plastic" and easily impressed with new information. The autistic child, on the other hand, is resistive and appears impervious to people and communication. He is unable to learn from speech models and does not search them out, attend to them, or anticipate their value in comfort, approval, help, or play. Once the attending behavior or an interactional set is established, closer to normal reception of language may be built. However, even after extensive receptive language development has occurred an autistic child may have unusual expressive language problems which are resistant to change, even with consistent input and an ability to code it appropriately. The autistic child may show inappropriate output. For example, when an autistic child was asked to subtract four cents from ten cents, he responded, "I'll draw a hexagon." This indicated he had the message and the computational skill but still showed inappropriate output.

The autistic child has difficulty generalizing language from past experience to different situations. This "literalness" or concreteness is exemplified by a child who could not generalize "down" to mean other than "on the floor."

Differential diagnosis of autism from other similar disorders is a tenuous matter at best. Autism, brain injury, retardation, childhood schizophrenia, severe childhood aphasia, congenital deafness, and cognitive delays show many striking language and speech similarities. The key differentiating factor between autism and the usual brain damage syndromes would appear to be the absence in the former of a history of a pre-, para-, or postnatal condition which would result in brain damage as well as the absence of objective neurological findings and the differences in interpersonal relationships. In differentiating between childhood schizophrenia and autism the critical factor is seen as being the age of onset; autism is a disorder whose symptoms are present very early in life while childhood schizophrenia includes only those cases whose disordered behavior manifests itself after an initial period of normal development. Both congenital deafness and aphasia may resemble autism. However, the history of an autistic child's disturbance in interpersonal relationships and other behavioral differences distinguish the autistic child from the aphasic and the congenital deaf child. In differentiating mental retardation and autism there are differences in affective relations, in motor development, and language development.

A speech and language pathologist cannot telescope his or her sights only to a child's language. Aspects of performance in cognitive, motor, affective and general communication skills should be considered in evaluating an autistic child. Speech and language are important pieces which together with others can complete the puzzle the child presents to an evaluation team.

Pediatrics*

Working with any handicapped children can be difficult for a pediatrician, but the autistic child may present the biggest challenge because of a lack of communication between the child and the physician.

At ISMRRD the process of pediatric evaluation of all children has certain features: first, all important previous medical records are gathered and studied; next, the family is interviewed to obtain the rest of the medical history; then the child is examined; and, finally, the pediatrician meets with all other professionals who have evaluated the child to compile all findings (including physical, social, psychological, and educational) and to make composite recommendations.

Although the framework for evaluation is basically the same for all children seen at ISMRRD, different techniques are utilized for the child known or suspected to be autistic.

*The Pediatrics section was written by Virginia Nelson, M.D., Acting Program Director for Pediatrics, ISMRRD.

First, the medical history is obtained from records and the parent(s) without the child present. This is done so the child is not discussed in his or her presence. Although all parents should probably be interviewed without their child present, this is especially crucial when it is impossible to know what the child can understand (or misunderstand).

Next, the child is observed in the examination room with his or her parents present. Much information can be gathered from this, including behavior in an unfamiliar setting, activity level in a small but crowded room when no demands for performance are made, general state of physical health and development, and gross and fine motor coordination.

Third, the general physical and neurologic examinations are conducted with special attention directed toward looking for indicators of organic, not psychological, dysfunction. Neurologic soft signs may be present. Rather than pointing to a specific area of involvement or lesion, soft signs are nonspecific—perhaps clumsiness or poor fine motor coordination.

Finally, an attempt is made to try to get the child to relate either to the examiner or parent on some simple task, such as hand-games (imitation of activities like finger-to-nose or rapidly alternating motion), gross motor activities, or self-dressing.

From the history and observations the following conclusions are drawn: (1) the child's usual state of health; (2) the presence or absence of neurologic dysfunction such as seizures, motor problems, or soft signs; (3) a characterization of the child's behavior in one particular setting. A diagnosis of autism is not made by the pediatrician, though its possibility is suggested in the conclusions, when the child has features suggestive of it. Recommendations for treatment of the behavior problems are not made by the pediatrician, but are decided in conjunction with the psychologist, psychiatrist, social worker, and others involved in evaluations of the child and family.

Many physicians prefer not to treat autistic children. Although seeing these children may be unpleasant at times, certain techniques help to keep outbursts to a minimum. First, the autistic child is a child first and not just a problem. Hence, he or she should be treated gently and with respect. Next, gather as much information as possible by observation of the child before intruding into his or her world. Then very gently intrude, allowing the child to look at instruments before using them and examining the child wherever the child is most comfortable (on the parent's lap, the floor, a chair, etc.). Finally, make demands on the child for performance if this is a necessary part of your exam.

Psychology*

One of the major problems in the psychological diagnosis of autism is that the diagnosis is based purely on external symptomatology. The usual internal psychological cues are unavailable because of the relative lack of almost any personal engagement or interchange on the child's part. The only other condition which can equal the paucity of communication cues is profound retardation in a deaf-blind child. In fact, even in stereotypes of behavior the autistic child resembles the profoundly retarded and deaf-blind child, with the exception that, although the autistic child, like the blind child, does not seem to fix his or her eyes on people or objects, it is clear that voluntary movement within the environment is that of a sighted person.

Another important diagnostic problem for psychology is the lack of agreement among investigators in the field of autism as to the nosological group of conditions to which it belongs. Language does not seem to be a relational tool in which the child conveys or processes experiences. He or she does not seem to be using speech for a back and forth flow between self and other selves, and there seems little comprehension of the speech of others. Even in those autistic children who have some language comprehension there is often a marked concreteness in the child's understanding.

In the cognitive area, both in perceptual difficulties and in the intelligence areas, the autistic child resembles the retarded child. More clinicians are finding autistic children testable on intelligence tests such as the Cattell Infant test, or the Gesell Infant test, or the Cattell-Binet. Some use the Bayley Mental Development tests to get at patterns of performances and patterns of strengths and weaknesses. I find the various form boards and pegboards useful and sometimes employ many of the Binet items in a play situation to get some indication of the level and quality of intelligence which may be operating. Often demonstrating the items and saying "Do this" can be effective in getting the child to cooperate. Likewise, watching the child for a response when he completes a task correctly or incorrectly is useful. For example, one autistic child I tested often laughed when he made an error, indicating he knew this was incorrect. Although most clinicians who work with complex diagnostic problems in the developmental disabilities now believe that autistic children are testable, it is an awesome, time-consuming task. Even after complet-

*The Psychology section was written by William Rhodes, Ph.D., Program Director of Psychology, ISMRRD.

ing a standardized test with a reliable score, it is necessary to interpret the validity of that score and the subtest responses. Although investigators are developing a consensus that retardation often accompanies autism, anyone who has engaged autistic children in long-term therapy or psychoeducational treatment has rich evidence from occasional flashes of behavior that there is much more intellectual capacity in many of these children than is accessible to testing.

A good medical history and a good social history is very important in arriving at the diagnosis. Since autism is a condition which has its onset very early it is important to establish developmental milestones and to get a picture of the child's early contributions to the emotional climate in the family. It has been my experience with most autistic children that their social-emotional behavior has been puzzling from infancy and that their pattern of development has been confusing to parents. Frequently, because of the many problems having an autistic child creates, some form of family intervention or support may be necessary.

In terms of medical history and examination, autistic children have more signs of neuropathology and are frequently below "normal" children in height and even weight. There are high incidences of prenatal, perinatal, and postnatal abnormalities.

As already indicated, two of the most outstanding characteristics in autism are extreme lack of social learning and failure to learn adaptive skills in school. In psychological evaluation of the child it is very important to assign a learning or evaluative task to the mother, and then to the father, to administer to the child. Not only can the evaluator have a sample of the parents' teaching style, but much can be observed and inferred from the interaction. In the same vein, it is good to have a sample of the teacher's style of teaching the child. With these three figures interacting with the child around a teaching or testing situation, one can not only see how the child learns or fails to learn with different adult figures, but one can also assess one's own interactive data obtained in the evaluation. For these reasons in a psychological evaluation I usually have the parents administer portions of various tests.

The psychologist should include his or her own reactions to the child in the evaluative data. In working with these children a medley of emotions are elicited. One feels frustrated, angry, inadequate, and sympathetic all at the same time. This child gives you only the barest hint of leads to follow in getting to his or her internal life. The tester experiences, in microcosm, the sense of relational futility experienced by all of the significant people in the child's environment.

These experiences of the child can be placed alongside the data provided in the social interview with the parents, and one can catch a glimpse of the parent's history with the child. One experiences frustration even in trying to find objects or aspects of the environment to which the child will relate. Frequently it is whirling, spinning, or turning objects. The child will often show some response to music and musical instruments, to stereotyped water play, to light switches, to latches, etc. Any insistence on mimicry or imitation in play or task activities is usually met with resistance, an absence of eye fixation, an absence of collaborative interest or emotions. The child not only withdraws and holds back, he or she seems constantly bent on escape. The evaluator feels like an intrusive jailer.

In summary, the autistic child is a puzzling problem in diagnosis. He or she resembles the retarded child, the deaf-blind child, the child with organic brain damage, or perceptual and psychoneurological anomalies, and frustrates the psychological tester in the assessment effort. The diagnostic problem is further complicated by the tester's own choice of causal frameworks, nosological categories, time of onset, and research data regarding autism.

Psychiatry

Most child psychiatric evaluations are based on three different inputs: (1) the history as related by the parents; (2) observation of the child; (3) personal interaction with the child. Depending on the type of disturbance, one may gain much information from one aspect but little from another. For example, in assessing a very fearful, anxious child who cries and screams when the psychiatrist makes any attempt to talk or play with the child, one has to rely heavily on history and observation to make a diagnosis. The history is most important in defining the general area of a possible disturbance and thus sets the parameters for a differential diagnosis. For example, from the history one can speculate that the child may be retarded or autistic, or shows another psychotic disturbance. However, based on the history, one can generally rule out a less severe problem such as a neurosis or a personality trait disturbance. In seeing a possibly autistic child, after determining what is the major reason for the referral and getting an idea of the concept of the problem, one determines associated symptoms. For example, with an autistic child the chief complaint may be a lack of speech development. It is then important to determine if there is no speech or limited speech or unusual speech or non-communicative speech, etc.

From the early history it is important to determine if there were problems during pregnancy and delivery or abnormalities in the early developmental milestones (when the child smiled, cooed, sat up, crawled, walked, etc.).

Personality and interpersonal relations are important to determine. Here one would stress how the child interacts with the parents, with his toys, and with the environment in general. Is the child withdrawn? Does he like to play alone? Does he follow mother around or does he avoid interaction? Does he show eye contact? Does he gesture when he wants something and cannot express it? Does he show unusual motions; for example, flapping, spinning, etc.? How does he respond to stimuli—are there unusual sensitivities? In giving this information, much of the material will be given by the parents spontaneously. Often one only needs to clarify certain points by asking for examples.

After getting a history, one should observe the child. How does he separate from parents? Does he explore the play room? Does he pick out any toys? How does he play with the toys—is the play stereotypic or does the play fit the function of the toy?

Finally the psychiatrist interacts with the child. This can be done on the verbal level or through play or both. In very withdrawn children, all one may be able to do is to see if the child will show eye contact or will sit on the examiner's lap or will accept a toy when it is handed to him. Often it is useful to bring the parents in and see how the child greets them. Will he look at them? Does he run to them? Will he play with them?

Infantile autism may occasionally be confused with other childhood disturbances. If we postulate that the initial referral problem is a lack of speech development, the differential diagnosis would include the following conditions—retardation, hearing loss, psychosocial deprivation, elective mutism, and various types of psychosis.

RETARDATION

In differentiating the retarded from the autistic child, several major factors should be addressed. From the history of the retarded child, developmental delays in areas other than language are often noted, such as motor development—sitting, walking, etc. Usually the retarded child may not understand something, but he can gesture or mimic, and appears to want to communicate. Overall interpersonal relations are not grossly impaired. He smiles at people, tries to please, and shows eye contact. He may, however, show some of the same unusual motor movements (flapping, etc., temper tantrums and responsiveness to pain or self-stimulations) seen in autistic children. It should also be kept in mind that sometimes retardation is not present at birth but may be part of a degenerative disease. A disease of this type which has frequently caused controversy is Heller's disease. In this illness children show a normal development until about three or four years of age. At that time a regression occurs with a child showing a loss of self-help skills and interacting with people. Controversy concerning the syndrome relates to whether this constitutes one illness or several degenerative diseases. A difference here from autism, however, is that Heller's is a progressive disease and there is a period of normal development.

DEAFNESS

Deaf children may seem to act as if they were retarded or even autistic. Usually, however, the hearing loss is diagnosed by an audiologist or pediatrician and rarely is such a child sent to a psychiatrist. From the history one can assess if the child seems unresponsive to sound rather than unresponsive in general, i.e., does he react to sights, does he like to be cuddled, does he gesture to communicate, etc. Usually one can determine in evaluating a deaf child that he reacts to persons and environment but only fails to react to sounds.

DEPRIVATION

Severely deprived children may show retardation in general development. They may be less responsive to persons and environment. Other delays, especially delays in speech, are frequent. Usually, however, some speech is present and this is normal but immature speech. Severe deprivation in the environment can readily be determined from the history. Another difference is that unlike retarded or autistic children, if the deprived child is placed in a normal healthy environment, much improvement is noted, and eventually the deprived child will be functioning at close to normal level.

ELECTED MUTISM

In this condition the child does speak but is mute in some circumstances. Most often around four or five years the child shows an unwillingness to talk in strange situations or to strangers. Typically this child speaks well at home but not at school. Again history and observation can accurately separate this type of child from the autistic.

OTHER PSYCHOSES

In this group one should include symbiotic psychosis and childhood schizophrenia. Symbiotic psychosis was first described by Margaret Mahler. Such children cling to mother seemingly as if they are an extension of her. They do not show the unresponsiveness typical of the autistic. Likewise the child showing childhood schizophrenia (whether it is or is not a separate entity) does not show the same unresponsiveness or delays typical of the autistic child. Often these other groups of children can use language, but the ideas they express are bizarre and unusual. These strange ideas are also often the basis for compulsive acts which are different from the stereotypic behavior of autistic children. For example, a schizophrenic, six-year-old child flushed the toilet many times during the day, yet seemed fearful to flush it after using the toilet. Once in therapy he explained he did this to reassure himself he would not be "swallowed up" by the toilet. Such types of fantasies are usually not expressed by autistic children.

As described, several psychiatric conditions may show certain similarities to autism, but a careful evaluation can usually adequately separate these from autism. However, if possible a comprehensive evaluation with other disciplines is desirable. This is done not only to make a diagnosis but to assess the child's skills and weaknesses so that a prescriptive plan can be worked out.

In summary the foregoing multi-disciplinary discussions of diagnosis show different approaches as well as overlapping areas. Often it is these areas common to several disciplines that provoke controversies, since differences of opinion can readily exist. Although we have our share of such controversies at the Institute for the Study of Mental Retardation and Related Disabilities we found simply talking out diagnostic or management disagreements works exceedingly well. Possibly having worked together on many cases is helpful, but the critical factor is the fact that the team members respect and recognize the need for input from other team members. By viewing a child from different perspectives we can provide the best service—and to do that we must work cooperatively. If more agencies tried such team approaches better service to the autistic child and family would be provided. There would be no less discussion, but the controversies would be resolved between professionals, and the parents would not be placed in the position of having to choose which advice to follow.

3

ETIOLOGY

BEFORE presenting any theory on etiology it is important to mention the authors' perspective so the reader can judge if inadvertently bias has been inserted in presenting various concepts on etiology.

Current research has demonstrated the etiology of autism as an organic impairment. The cause of this impairment is unknown, but several different "causes" may produce the fundamental central nervous system defect which gives rise to the symptoms of autism. Furthermore we feel that early investigations focusing on parents as the culprits in the etiology of autism has led to a number of serious problems in the general area of study. First, this concept has produced much guilt and defensiveness in parents of autistic children. Second, not infrequently because of this view provision of services has been delayed or the services provided were inadequate in terms of the "real" problem. Third, because of the justifiable anger on the part of the parents and the defensiveness on the part of professionals a rift has developed between parents and professionals. These aspects will be discussed in greater detail in later chapters, but it is important to keep these factors in mind when discussing the etiology of autism.

PSYCHOGENIC BASIS

Kanner's initial description of autism triggered a major "nature or nurture" controversy. His description of the parents of autistic children as highly intelligent, well-educated, and usually undemonstrative and detached stimulated speculation about this environmental factor being the crucial aspect or the "cause" of the illness. Kanner himself has refuted this notion saying that he felt a major factor was a biological one; nonetheless, he also described an interplay of heredity and environment: "regardless of the problems of heredity and constitution, life experiences

45

have confused these children, made normal relationships impossible, and driven them to withdrawal and schizophrenic behavior" (Kanner 1957).

The strongest supporters of the theory of environmental causation have been several researchers and clinicians who, from a psychoanalytic perspective, have explained autistic behavior as a reactive deviant form of development. Bruno Bettelheim and Frances Tustin have written books on autism viewing this condition from such a perspective. Both their concepts will be presented as examples of approaching autism from a psychodynamic point of view.

In her book *Autism and Childhood Psychosis* (1973), Tustin discusses the early infant stage as normal primary autism. The baby experiences sensations but is unaware of his body parts and does not recognize a boundary of self and non-self; that is, the baby is unaware of mother being separate from the baby. Most mothers do not over-react by anticipating the infant's every want, nor do most mothers reject the baby, leaving him with excessive frustration. Gradually, with maternal support, the baby begins to differentiate his own body parts, sees himself as separate from mother, and differentiates between people and things. This early stage of development stressing the child's lack of awareness of anything outside himself and the importance of mother, especially mother-child relationship around breast feeding, has been generally accepted as part of normal child development for a long time. This stage is sometimes called the oral phase, trust vs. mistrust stage, anaclytic or primary narcissism. Tustin refers to this stage of development as *"normal primary autism,"* differentiating it from an abnormal prolongation of this stage leading to pathological autism. Tustin feels that abnormal primary autism results when the normal early stage of development is prolonged either because the child experiences a gross lack or a partial lack of nurturing.

Tustin proposes another form of autism which she terms "encapsulated secondary autism." This type of autism results when the child experiences separateness from the mother too early; not being ready for this, the child is traumatized by this sensation of separateness. In order not to experience this frightening over-separateness, the child shuts out the "not-me" part of the world, and, in effect, creates a barrier between himself and the outside world.

Bruno Bettelheim also sees autism as arising out of the infant's early life experiences. In *The Empty Fortress* (1967), he describes how infants are active and give signals, especially in relation to breast feeding. If the child is frustrated and feels there is nothing he can do about an unpredictable and/or unresponsive world, he may become autistic. This may occur in the first 6 months if the child's activity is blocked in general, or it can occur around 6-9 months when the child attempts to relate to others and this is blocked. Finally, autism can result if between 18 months and 2 years, the child is blocked in "his active efforts to master the world physically and intellectually" (p. 47). In repressing all activity and with it repressing hostility at the outside world, the child withdraws into fantasy and into autism. Bettelheim states that organic factors may be present in the development of autism, but parental attitudes allow for these factors to lead to autism in some children, yet not in others. He feels "in all cases known to us . . . parental attitudes . . . were experienced by the child as the wish he did not exist."

From these examples cited to support the psychogenic origin of autism, we can readily understand why many parents of autistic children may have felt frustrated, guilty, and frequently hostile to professionals. Explanations that parental attitudes may be unconscious, and thus not deliberate, did not help the situation. Parents were frequently suspicious that whenever a professional took a family history or other data it was to be "used against them." Despite this damaging effect, a word in the defense of those who subscribe to the notion of a psychogenic origin must be inserted. In the early studies—especially Kanner's samples of autistic children—there was a high incidence of upper socioeconomic, intellectual parents. This group may have had more access to special clinics such as Kanner's. Studies have also shown that in describing conditions of children, a child from the lower socioeconomic group is more likely to be diagnosed as retarded, whereas one coming from a higher socioeconomic group is more likely to be diagnosed as emotionally disturbed. Even if this may account for the correlation of autism with higher socioeconomic status, such explanations could not be accepted on face value. Other factors, including that these parents were somehow instrumental in the etiology, had to be investigated. In observing a phenomenon scientists explain it in terms of a working hypothesis and reject the hypothesis only if additional data proves it incorrect. For these reasons researchers speculated on the etiology of autism as being related to the child's environment even if this avenue of investigation was painful to many parents.

In addition to the works described above other researchers theorized a psychogenic origin. Some suggested a lack of stimulation, a lack of parental warmth, or intrapsychic conflict resulting from deviant family interaction. In the late 1960s and 70s, however, systematic investigations exploring such factors showed that parents of autistic children had no specific common personality traits, and no unusual environmental stresses or specific family patterns could be found. Furthermore, follow-up studies done on numerous children who were neglected and rejected have shown these children usually do well once they are placed in a different environment. Autistic children, however, show no significant change in a different environment. Thus one must conclude environment is of little significance in the development of this condition.

Although not all the possibilities of a psychogenic origin have been explored, Rutter (1974) notes that "there is so much evidence *against* the view that autism is a primarily psychogenic disorder that it would not seem worthwhile to investigate it further." It must be emphasized, however, that even if autism does not appear to be due to psychogenic factors the parents and the home environment are extremely important in working with these children; in a later chapter this aspect will be discussed in some detail.

An etiology which proposes a psychological origin coupled with a neurological deficit has been suggested by Ward in *Childhood Autism and Structural Therapy* (1976). This hypothesis proposes that the mother's anxiety during pregnancy produces a child who is slower in his sensory development. As a result of maternal anxiety neuro-endocrinological changes occur in the mother which effect neural, endocrine, or other structures in the fetus. Later on, mothers cannot meet the special needs of such a child and autism results. Ward found that mothers of autistic children in retrospect reported a high incidence of stress during the pregnancy either because of emotional problems, stress within the family, or some other significant difficulty. It is well known that mothers who have handicapped children later search for problems during pregnancy and delivery. In order to explain the handicap it would be necessary to do progressive studies or devise some method of evaluating anxiety during pregnancy in a more objective manner than this method which relies on the mother's perception and recall. Also, as maternal anxiety has not been demonstrated to cause abnormalities in the fetus, it would be necessary to show that anxiety in the mother indeed produces excess epinephrine or another substance which has a negative effect on fetal development. Thus this theory, like the preceding ones, cannot be readily accepted. Nevertheless, research in the area of abnormalities during pregnancy as related to autism is an important one and will need to be pursued.

BIOGENIC BASIS

In addition to the negative results exploring the possibility of a psychogenic basis in autism, there have been several indications of a biogenic origin. The fact that autism is present so early in life is in itself suggestive of a biological problem. Autism has been linked to conditions which produce central nervous system (CNS) impairment. Although perinatal complications have not been clearly linked to autism, rubella (German measles) during pregnancy does cause a higher incidence of autism in the offspring (Chess 1971). It is well known that rubella causes a number of other congenital abnormalities including those effecting the CNS— namely, deafness, mental deficiency, and microcephaly. Thus it is not unreasonable to suspect that rubella may cause other CNS impairment which can manifest as autism. Other conditions in children which affect the CNS such as meningitis, encephalitis, tuberous sclerosis, and phenylketonuria have been reported to be associated with autistic patterns of behavior.

When autistic children are evaluated and followed, they frequently show some signs of neurological dysfunction. In terms of intelligence, most though not all autistic children show IQs below the average range (below 80). EEG studies done on autistic children have shown abnormalities even in those children who do not demonstrate a seizure disorder clinically (Tanguay 1976). As already mentioned, epilepsy is more common in autistic than in normal children, becoming frequently evident clinically in adolescence or young adulthood. In one study, a quarter of the autistic adolescents and young adults showed seizures some time in their lives (Rutter 1970).

Various soft neurological signs have been described at times with autistic children. Soft signs refer to neurological abnormalities which do not pinpoint a specific area of neurological damage (the lesion cannot be localized by these signs). Such signs are often associated with CNS damage or dysfunction. Mobility problems such as toe-walking or hand flapping may be viewed in this category. Various perceptual inconsistencies found in autistic children are examples of this type of problem.

As more research was done in the biological area, various theories arose as to the exact nature of the biological problem in autism. Before discussing some of these conditions, it should be mentioned that we know from other conditions how different etiologies produce similar symptoms. One agent may produce different symptoms under different circumstances. For example, rubella infection in pregnant women may cause deafness in one baby, retardation in another, and cataracts in still another, or all three of these conditions may be found in a single infant. In another situation, various causes may be responsible for producing the same condition. In retardation, the etiology may be hereditary (Tay-Sachs disease), genetic in origin but not necessarily hereditary (Down's syndrome), metabolic (hypothyroidism, Cretinism), infectious (post encephalitis), traumatic. Even with all these specific etiologies the majority of cases of retardation are of unknown origin.

With regard to autism, then given there are indications of a biological etilogy and also given autism may be associated with other conditions, it is reasonable to suspect there may be more than one "cause"; that is, several different conditions may produce pathological changes which are manifested as the syndrome of autism. If this is true, then the damage should occur in the same area in order to produce the same symptoms. Following this line of reasoning, a number of researchers have attempted to specify where such a lesion or disturbance of normal function could occur. In considering the etiology of autism, one must consider what agents may be involved as well as the abnormality this agent produces which gives rise to the syndrome of autism.

Various researchers have proposed several possible biogenic agents or types of abnormalities which could cause pathological changes producing the symptoms of autism. Three of the more promising areas of consideration are genetic, biochemical, and viral.

Genetic

The possibility of a chromosomal abnormality in autism has been explored. Such chromosomal studies have shown no abnormalities in autistic children.

Each chromosome carries many genes which transmit information to the cell. Unlike the chromosomes, genes cannot be visualized directly. An abnormal or mutant gene can often be identified because that same gene will duplicate itself and transmit a changed message not only to the cells of that individual but also to subsequent generations inheriting the gene. Thus, by taking a genetic history of a disorder, one can often determine a pattern of inheritance. One other aspect of gene regulation is important to mention before trying to relate the above information to autism. Though still speculative, one of the theories of control of gene action suggests a feedback mechanism from the cell and cell products. Thus, an interaction may exist between the gene and its environment.

Returning now to the consideration of autism and genes, we could speculate that autism is a disorder inherited as an autosomal dominant, an autosomal recessive, or a sex-linked condition. An autosomal dominant condition is one where only one of the pair of genes of that autosomal chromosome pair need be mutant to produce the condition. If one parent has the condition, one-half of the children can be expected to inherit it. Obviously, this is not true in autism. In an autosomal recessive condition both copies of the gene must be mutant to produce the condition. In this instance, if one parent has the condition, one-quarter of the children can be expected to inherit the disorder. Phenylketonuria (PKU) is this type of genetic disorder as are several other metabolic disorders. In these disorders, however, a much stronger familial tendency is seen than that in autism. The sex-linked hypothesis is a type of genetic abnormality which can be ruled out in autism because the ratio of males to females would have to be much greater (this ratio can be computed from the occurrence of a condition in the population).

From the above discussion, we can see that autism is unlikely to be the result of a simple hereditary condition, but there is some indication of a familial tendency in autism. From a number of studies of families of autistic children, it was estimated that there is a 2 percent chance of another child being autistic (rather than 4/10,000 as in the general population). In a recent study of 78 autistic children, 8 percent had a relative who was also autistic (Colman 1976). A review of twin studies indicates a higher concordant rate for autism in monozygotic twins than dizygotic twins (Rimland 1964). Thus, even though it is unlikely that autism is inherited as a single gene abnormality, other genetic possibilities need to be explored. For example, autism could be the result of a multiple gene abnormality, meaning that in order for the condition to be present, several genes must be of the mutant variety. Or, possibly, several different genes can cause the same abnormality. These possibilities have not been explored completely. The possibility that autism is caused by multiple factors with the genetic factor being one necessary aspect has likewise not been explored.

Biochemical

Most of the biochemical investigations in autism have been concerned with neurotransmitters, though a few other types of biochemical studies have also been done. The neurotransmitters can be viewed as chemical mediators which affect muscular contraction and nerve activity. These mediators have been investigated in a number of psychiatric conditions such as depression and schizophrenia, since it is known they affect moods, emotions, and thought processes. A mediator's excess or deficiency or even an imbalance between two different mediators may cause disturbed behavior. Though several neurotransmitters have been studied in adults, seratonin has been focused on in autistic children.

Seratonin is a product of the metabolism of an essential amino acid

—tryptophan. It is called essential because it is indispensable to humans, yet the body cannot synthesize it from other protein. For this reason it must be part of the individual's diet. Chemically, seratonin resembles LSD, but unlike LSD, seratonin is a naturally occurring substance found in high concentrations in certain parts of the brain and other parts of the body such as intestinal mucosa and blood platelets. Seratonin appears to be necessary for normal brain function. In studies of adults both when the levels of seratonin are decreased (by taking LSD or the drug reserpine) or when the levels of seratonin are increased, behavioral abnormalities may be seen. Despite interesting research data indicating high levels of seratonin in some autistic children, in evaluating seratonin levels, there are numerous problems and conflicting results.

Because of conflicting results obtained, this area might seem unworthy of further consideration. Yet, when we examine another aspect of seratonin research, it suddenly seems very important. Studies of seratonin levels in hyperactive children have shown a low level of seratonin in whole blood. Furthermore, the low level approached normal levels when the children showed clinical improvement.

Thus, if hyperkinetic children show an improvement when seratonin levels in their blood rose closer to a normal level, possibly in autistic children an improvement could be seen if the seratonin level was decreased to approximately normal levels. This might be done by using drugs. Or, since seratonin is a product of trytophan, dietary restriction of this protein could decrease the seratonin level. Of course, much more research needs to be done in this area—laboratory techniques must be perfected and patients must be closely monitored. Nevertheless, seratonin appears to be important in the search for an etiology and management of autism, and it will be discussed further under therapy.

Other biochemical studies are sparse and though technically not complex, analysis of the data might be difficult. For example, in a study by Colman et al. (1976), 67 autistic children were evaluated for such things as the level of uric acid in blood and urine. Uric acid is a product of the breakdown of cells, particularly the cell nuclei. Typically, it is elevated in leukemia and gout, but it has also been reported increased in some mentally retarded individuals. Even though in this study 22 percent of the autistic children showed elevated uric acid in the urine (but not in the blood), the significance of this data is difficult to interpret.

Biochemical defects may be produced not only by abnormalities of metabolism but also by inadequate intake of necessary substances or by malabsorption. One type of a malabsorption syndrome is celiac disease, characterized by dietary intolerance to fat and gluten (found in wheat).

In this disease, it is believed gluten may injure intestinal epithelium. The disease is characterized by bulky stools of unabsorbed fat and other substances (steatorrhea), failure to grow, and other physical changes. In some children with this disease, emotional problems have been reported, and several autistic children have been identified as having celiac disease (Colman 1976). In one child reported to have autism and celiac disease, a decrease in autistic symptoms was seen when the child was placed on a gluten-free diet (Goodwin and Goodwin 1969). In an evaluation of 78 autistic children, 10 percent showed celiac disease (Colman 1976). However, as those investigators point out, the presence of two conditions in the same patient does not necessarily mean that one condition causes the other. For example, the two conditions could have a similar genetic basis and thus perhaps be associated with each other. Still, the possibility of a causative effect exists and will need to be explored in future studies.

Generally, the area of investigating biochemical abnormalities in children is fraught with many technical problems and difficulties in assessing the significance of the data; yet this avenue of research into the possible causes for autism continues to be important.

Viral

Some viral infections during pregnancy have been known to cause serious damage in the developing fetus. As mentioned earlier, rubella (German measles) in pregnancy can cause a number of congenital abnormalities. Autism has also been found in some children who had been infected with the virus during pregnancy. In one study of 64 children with congenital rubella, eight were described as autistic (Desmond 1970). In another study of 243 children with congenital rubella, ten showed autism and another eight showed some symptoms of autism (Chess 1971). The incidence of autism in these groups is much higher than 4/10,000 found in the general population. Thus it appears that rubella CNS damage may produce the syndrome of autism. It may be argued that congenital rubella does not cause the damage, but rather autism in such cases arises as a secondary syndrome related either to the mental retardation or sensory deprivation resulting from deafness or blindness found in some congenital rubella children. This does not appear to be the case. Autism is a specific syndrome which may be present in children who also are retarded or are blind or deaf, but as was discussed previously it does not arise secondarily to these defects.

Following the idea of viral infections being causative in autism, other investigators have explored other viral infections. In a study on the association of herpes and autism (Colman 1976), it was found that a group of autistic children showed a higher incidence of antibodies for oral herpes (cold sores). Whether this means the children showed a higher titer of antibodies because of exposure to this virus in utero or for some reason had a lack of resistance and were more prone to be infected in their childhood could not be determined. It does appear, however, that this avenue of investigation in the search for an etiology will need to be pursued further.

From the above discussion on etiology it can be seen that many avenues are being explored to find a cause of autism. Because a number of these avenues have shown positive results some researchers propose there is no one cause. Rather, autism can occur as a result of a variety of biological impairments. Whether genetic, biochemical, viral, or another impairment is the original cause, a defect is produced in the CNS which gives rise to the symptoms of autism. These investigators suggest that autism, like mental retardation or learning disabilities, is a syndrome which can arise through various factors. All these different causes produce the same critical CNS impairment which in turn produces the symptoms characteristic of autism. In searching where such damage could be present researchers have evaluated autistic children from the perspective of soft neurological signs, abnormalities on EEGs, speech problems, characteristic learning patterns, and other variables. From such data several CNS types of impairments have been proposed.

In order to discuss some of the current thinking of the possible CNS defects in the development of autism, it is useful to review brain function in relation to psychological processes. The next few paragraphs will describe some general principles on perception, integration, and cognitive activity which can serve as background. A word of caution should be inserted here—most of the discussion is based on the interpretation of A. R. Luria, and it may be possible that other workers in this area have somewhat different interpretations. Furthermore, for the sake of simplicity much of this discussion will deal with broad issues rather than specifics and intricacies of function.

CENTRAL NERVOUS SYSTEM

In understanding mental processes, instead of considering localized areas of the brain (see Figures 1 and 2) such as areas receiving sensation from

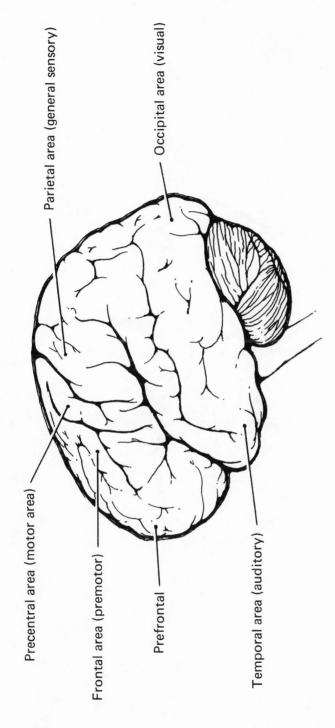

LATERAL VIEW

Parietal area (general sensory)

Occipital area (visual)

Precentral area (motor area)

Frontal area (premotor)

Prefrontal

Temporal area (auditory)

FIGURE 1   LEFT CEREBRAL HEMISPHERE SHOWING PORTIONS
OF SECONDARY AND TERTIARY FUNCTIONAL UNITS

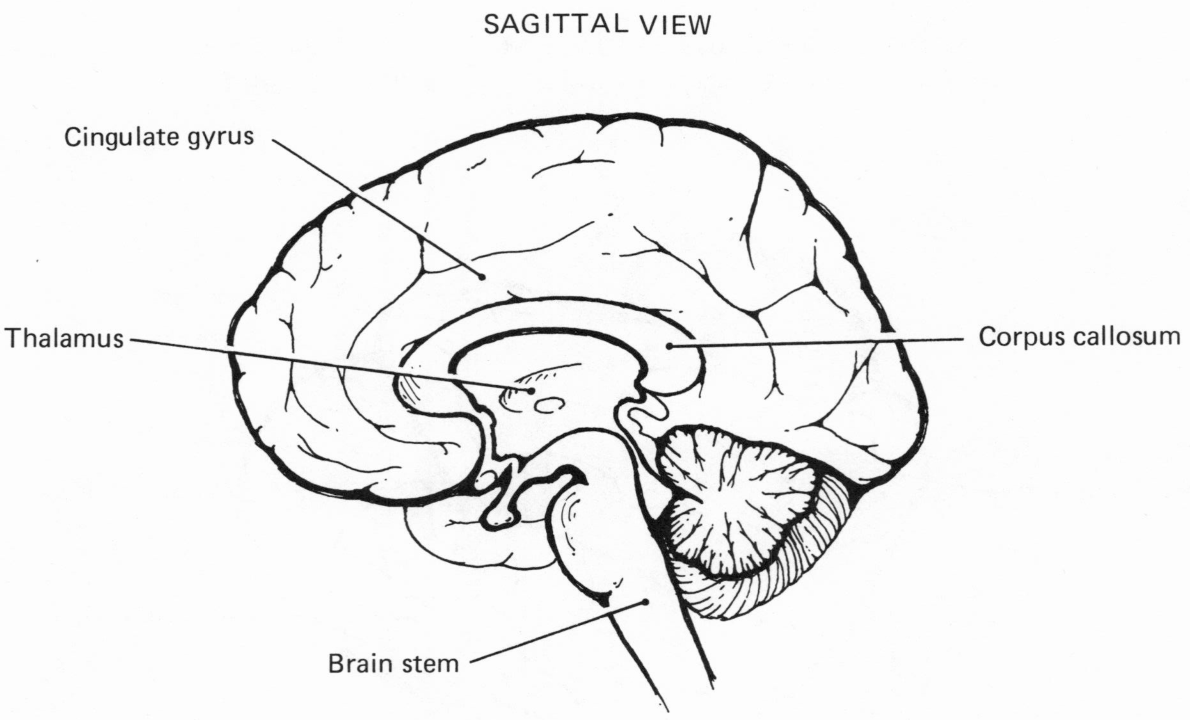

SAGITTAL VIEW

Corpus callosum

Cingulate gyrus

Thalamus

Brain stem

RIGHT CEREBRAL HEMISPHERE AND BRAIN STEM
SHOWING PORTIONS OF PRIMARY FUNCTIONAL UNIT

FIGURE 2

the arms or legs or areas sending out motor responses, it is more logical and more accurate to consider *functional* systems within the brain. We can identify three such functional units necessary for all mental activity: (1) a unit for regulating tone or waking; (2) a unit for obtaining, processing, and storing information; and (3) a unit for programming regulating and verifying mental activity.

Unit for Regulating Tone or Waking

This functional unit consists of the subcortex and brain stem (the brain stem is that portion of the brain connecting the spinal cord with the cerebrum and consists of the medulla, pons, mid-brain, and diencephalon). The most important activities of this system are general arousal and the activation and inhibition or, in other words, *the modulation* of impulses in their transmission to higher centers. There are two primary sources of these impulses. The first arises from *internal processes*. This includes metabolic processes connected with respiration, digestion, etc., as well as more complex instinctive systems such as food-getting or sexual behavior. The second source is the stimuli from the *outside world* arriving via sensory modalities such as touch, hearing, and vision. The sensory input source is not recognized at this level without additional input from higher centers. But when input from higher centers is received, it allows for comparing new stimuli to previous experiences so that if the sensation was experienced earlier, special mobilization of the organism is not necessary and the response may become automatic or habitual. Basically, then, this system regulates awakening and control over various sensory input to prevent over or under excitation and allows for habituation or automatic responses through input from cortical areas.

Unit for Receiving, Analyzing, and Storing Information

This unit is located primarily on the lateral aspects of the hemispheres including the visual (occipital), auditory (temporal), and general sensory (parietal) regions. Each of these areas is organized in three layers. The primary area is specific to that system; that is, the neurons in the visual area receive only visual stimulation, the neurons in the auditory receive only acoustic stimuli, etc. Thus, the primary area shows *high modal specificity* and there are no association fibers with other areas.

The secondary layer consists of various cells (this layer is less modal specific) and is adept in receiving stimuli from other areas. Both the secondary and tertiary areas are successively less modal specific each showing more association with other sensory areas than the previous layer.

These two layers are thus much more involved in integrating stimuli from other areas with the stimuli received from its own primary zone. In addition, the secondary and tertiary zones are involved in analyzing, synthesizing, and coding the information received.

The tertiary area in particular is adapted for conversion of concrete perception into abstract perception. In the secondary and tertiary zones of this second functional unit, sensory information is received from its own primary sensory unit. This information is integrated with that from other sensory units. The information is analyzed and coded and converted into abstract symbols.

Each area of the brain that forms the secondary functional unit is organized in the same manner. Thus, general sensation (parietal), auditory (temporal), and visual (occipital) areas are organized in the same hierarchical fashion with a primary area for reception of stimuli superimposed by a secondary zone and finally a tertiary zone.

Histologically, differences can be seen in these areas. In terms of development the tertiary layer which shows most association and least specificity is the last to develop. Another point should be made about the second functional unit; this unit as well as the third functional unit shows a progressive lateralization in the three zones. The functions of the primary zone are identical in both hemispheres, but the secondary and tertiary zones show lateralization in that the left hemisphere (in right-handed persons) becomes dominant. This hemisphere plays an essential role in speech.

Unit for Programming, Regulation, and Verification of Activity

The third functional unit is primarily concerned with organization of conscious activity. The second unit as described is largely an afferent (incoming) system concerned with receiving and integrating information. This third unit, however, is basically an efferent (outgoing) system involved in creating intentions, plans, and regulating behavior according to those plans. Also, this system verifies conscious activity by comparing it with the original intentions. Basically, this functional unit is located anteriorly in the hemispheres and includes the motor cortex as well as the frontal lobes. Like the second functional unit, this unit also shows a hierarchical arrangement of more complex layers. These layers are not superimposed on each other but are adjacent to each other.

The primary zone in this area is the motor cortex. This area sends out impulses to the body, causing motor action. The secondary zone, which is the organizer and synthesizer for action, is the premotor area.

The most important and most complex area is the tertiary zone, which consists primarily of the prefrontal area. The prefrontal area has numerous connections with various parts of the brain including the brain stem. It receives many afferent fibers and sends out efferent fibers; thus much synthesis of impulse can take place here, and organization and regulation can be transmitted out.

This area is very important in speech and other human activity. In animals the prefrontal area is small, but in man this area occupies up to a quarter of the total mass of the hemispheres. It is the last brain area to develop in man and does not mature completely in children until 4–7 years. In adults, lesions in this area have been observed to cause disturbances in speech, particularly in the use of speech to modify behavior. Analyzing of information is impaired with the person fixating on one detail and responding to that rather than the total. Even tasks involving visual analysis are impaired in such a person.

At this point, it may seem as if the foregoing discussion on mental processes was aimed to show that autistic children have an impairment in the prefrontal area of the brain. This is probably true, but it would be erroneous to assume this is the primary or causative defect in autism. In a developing organism, a defect in a lower area will probably cause some impairment in higher levels. As was described, the three functional areas show a hierarchical arrangement. Even within each functional unit this is true; each successive layer shows greater complexity and more association with other areas. In an adult, if a lesion occurs in one area, higher zones usually are not affected. In children, however, as we are dealing with a growing organism, each zone is necessary for development of the next higher zone. Thus, if primary zones are impaired, normal development of subsequent zones is interfered with. As was already mentioned, the third functional unit is not completely developed until about 7 years of age; thus a defect in a lower area is very likely to have some effect on the development of this most complex area of the brain.

With this background let us consider some of the prevalent theories of CNS defects in autism.

PERCEPTUAL INCONSTANCY

Ornitz and Ritvo (1968) suggested that the underlying problem of autism is a disturbance of modulation or perception. This involves overexcitation alternating with overinhibition of sensory input, unusual preference for some sensory receptors over other receptors, and difficulties in interpreting internal sensations. Because of these perception problems the child cannot gain a stable concept of himself and his environment. Because of the primary problem in integrating sensory input, the child secondarily does not learn to interact normally with others or to use communicative speech. These investigators point to the unusual sensory sensitivities of autistic children as well as experimental data to support their hypothesis. As pointed out earlier, these children may show no response to a loud noise but be extremely sensitive to faint sounds such as the rustling of paper. Visual sensation may show inconstancies in that the autistic child will totally ignore some persons or objects yet be fascinated by minute details of his own hands, fingers, or other objects. Some autistic children show unusual preferences for some sensory receptors and not others. Usually, auditory and visual sensory stimuli are ones most people react to, but autistic children frequently show a preference for touch, smell, and taste. Again, in these sensory modalities autistic children may show a preference for one type of texture (or smell or taste) but react very negatively to another. For example, an autistic child may stroke a smooth velvet surface but react with anger at having to touch a rough surface.

It has been postulated that these inconstancies are related to a perception regulation defect possibly located in the brain stem. One such regulating system which has its nuclei in the brain stem is the vestibular system. The vestibular system coordinates reflexes of the eyes, neck, and body in maintaining equilibrium, and it has been suggested this system may be important in regulating more complex relationships between general sensory input and motor output.

Experiments on autistic children using vestibular stimulation have shown abnormalities in eye movements which were explained on the basis of abnormal interaction between light and vestibular stimuli. Other experiments showed differences on EEG during dreaming sleep (REM) in autistic and normal children. This, too, is supportive of the theory of perceptual inconstancy (Tanguay 1976).

Studies in a different area but related to this general concept have suggested that autistic children may have problems with regulation of heart rate related to brain stem regulation. Experimental evidence suggests regulation in the brain stem may be affected in autistic children (MacCulloch and Williams 1971).

As a result of the autistic child's inability to use sensory input to make perceptual discrimination, the child uses manipulation of objects and body motion to understand sensation. Thus, the twirling, hand flapping, positioning and posturing often seen in autistic children may be compensatory actions aimed at making sense out of defective perceptions. The apparent intolerance for change may be the child's attempt to maintain a perceptual set he can understand. Other peculiarities of behavior, such as seemingly unprovoked temper tantrums, can also be explained on the basis of overexcitation or overinhibition of systems that regulate sensory input. Because of a lack of equilibrium in perception or perceptual inconstancy, the child secondarily cannot relate to a world that either causes sensory overloading or underloading (with frequent alternating of both of these). He cannot gain an understanding of his own boundaries, nor can he learn to imitate or to relate to others.

If we refer back to the description of normal brain function, it can be seen that a defect in the primary functional unit (the unit concerned with tone, waking, and regulation of sensory input) can produce perceptual inconstancy as described by Ornitz and Ritvo.

CENTRAL COGNITIVE DEFECT

This theory focuses on the autistic child's impairment in abstract memory. Hermelin (1976) and others have suggested that in processing information received from sensory channels, normal children can extract redundancies and recognize appropriate rules to store such information; that is, they can code the information. Autistic children receive the sensory input but cannot extract crucial information. They retain the initial input in its precise or uncoded form. Since information must be coded into abstract memory in order to be both stored and retrieved, these children are unable to retain the information for long periods of time and can neither build nor modify this information in the way usual learning is accomplished. The information retained is short term, sensory specific, non-abstract information which is useful in order to recall precise locations of objects or to parrot back a phrase. However, without abstract coding normal memory as it is used in language and social interaction does not develop.

The supporters of this theory point to experimental evidence showing that autistic children, when compared to other groups of children, have greater difficulty in extracting rules, recognizing redundancies, and retaining information in any way other than rote memory.

If this theory is viewed from the standpoint of normal brain function, it can be seen that coding, storing, and retrieving information is a function of the second functional unit. The secondary and tertiary zones in this area are involved in integrating information received from the different sensory modalities, coding this information, and storing it. However, the third functional unit is also necessary in memory, since this unit is involved in active thinking. Without normal functioning of this unit, passive imprinting is possible; that is, the person can learn by rote memory but can neither plan nor take active steps to aid the memory process.

CROSS-MODAL ASSOCIATION DEFECT

DeMyer (1971) and others have pointed to defects in transfering information from one modality to another and problems in overselectivity in responding to stimuli. Normally, children are adept at receiving information in one sensory modality and responding in another. For example, when Johnny hears his name called he will respond "yes, coming," or run to the person calling him. Autistic children not only have difficulty in receiving an auditory cue and responding verbally but they show problems in transferring information from visual to motor, auditory to fine motor, and in other such transfers. This problem of cross-modal information processing has been investigated by a number of researchers who found in a variety of controlled studies that autistic children consistently have problems in receiving information in one modality and responding in another. Also, they appear to have problems in being overselective or unable to generalize from one modality to another. For example, if normal children are given a complex stimulus involving auditory, visual, and tactile cues they will soon generalize and on presentation of any one of the cues the response will occur. Autistic children, however, did not show this generalization. They either responded to all three cues or appeared to select one of the three and respond to that one, but not the other two.

Thus it appears autistic children may have problems in association areas of the central nervous system, particularly involving cross-modal associations. As was described under normal brain function, the unit most involved with association of different sensory modalities is the second functional unit. Specifically, the third zone of this unit allows for the various analyzers to work together. However, before deciding that only this unit would be involved in a cross-modal defect, it must be remembered that this unit is still under the control of the third functional unit.

LANGUAGE DEFECT

Rutter and a number of other investigators have suggested that the primary deficit of autistic children is an abnormality in the comprehension of language (Rutter *et al.* 1971). Several researchers in this area suggested that the mothers of autistic children serve as a poor model for their child, as these mothers have deficient speech. However, other studies have indicated that the mother's speech is largely dependent on the child's speech (Fraser & Roberts 1975). Therefore, any deficiencies in the speech of mothers of autistic children could be explained on the basis of the mother's reaction to an unresponsive child (Cantwell *et al.* 1977). Furthermore, there is directly conflicting data which indicates that mothers of autistic children are similar to mothers of normal children in the language they use with their children. Thus it appears that the theory of language deficiency in mothers of autistic children causing the autistic child's language problems is incorrect. Instead, the language deficit of autistic children is probably a developmental defect.

In exploring this issue, Rutter (1974) has postulated that autistic children are similar to children showing a receptive developmental language disorder. However, the autistic child's disorder is more severe, or as Rutter stated, "deeper (in that the impairment of comprehension was more severe) and also wider (in the impairment of gesture as well as of spoken and written language)."

To understand the implications of this, we should briefly discuss language and its importance. Speech and language are not synonymous. Many workers consider language to be a system of symbols, an abstract code that permits transmission of messages; gesture, for example, is a form of language. Speech, on the other hand, usually refers to the vocalization used to express words. Unfortunately, not all workers have the same definition, and even worse, not infrequently the terms "language" and "speech" are used interchangeably. This interchangeable use of terms is especially true of the translated works of A. R. Luria. While this is most likely a problem of translation, it can be confusing. Thus, for the purpose of this discussion, in order to minimize confusion, "language" has been substituted where appropriate for "speech," even if this was not the term used by the original writer or researcher. In this discussion not all aspects of language development or all of the research of language deficits in autistic children can be considered. Only those aspects crucial to the understanding of the language deficit as it pertains to the mechanism of development of autism will be discussed.

Babies respond to sound very early. Even in utero the fetus may move in response to a loud noise. Neonates likewise can make auditory discrimination, since in the newborn period babies have been shown to respond differently to different sounds. By 4–6 months, the baby coos, squeals, and makes other similar noises. In the next two or three months the baby learns to imitate some sounds and gestures. By 10 months most babies can play pat-a-cake and wave bye-bye. Although most children do not say their first words until 1 year, they can understand much and can also communicate by gesture. As mentioned earlier, autistic children do not communicate by gesture and typically do not imitate. The autistic child does hear, but he attends to sound on a selective basis; that is, he may listen to a particular sound but he does not attend to or focus on the object emitting the sound; he does not attend to a person speaking. Likewise, he does not understand language.

Closely connected with these problems and perhaps most critical is the autistic child's apparent inability to develop an "inner" language or verbal concepts in a symbolic way. In many speech disorders a child may not talk, but he has a concept of meaning. Even young children show this inner language. For example, a young child may not be able to say "cup," but he indicates he knows the meaning by drinking from it. Or he may babble to the receiver of a telephone, again indicating he is beginning to use symbolism and can match current events to past experience. Later a normal child will demonstrate inner language by playing imaginative games such as "school," "cops and robbers," or "house."

Autistic children do not show inner language. They do not use play items appropriately nor do they show imaginative play. As described earlier, most autistic children continue to have severe language problems in comprehension and expression throughout their lives. Because of these severe problems, Rutter and others have suggested the central mechanism in the development of autism may be a severe developmental disorder of language. The disorder is similar to aphasia, but broader. Aphasic children do not have such great problems with gesture, imitation, or inner language. It appears in autism that a global language disorder may be present which affects attending to language, comprehension, inner language, and of course expressive language.

If these aspects of language development are considered from the standpoint of brain function, the complexity of the problem as well as the importance of language to normal development becomes apparent.

Many modern concepts in neuropsychology and psycholinguistics are based on a view of language as not just a means of communication, but also a complex organized form of conscious activity. The basic structure of language—the word—is seen as consisting of complex multidimensional cues. Words provide certain stimuli through their meaning as well as sound and structure; even visual imagery and emotional reactions are evoked by words. Thus, the very basic unit of language—the word—is already complex.

Next, whether language is received or expressed, complex systems are involved. Receptive or impressive language first must be heard, next attended to, and subsequently decoded or analyzed into significant elements or phonemes. Then the analysis of the total meaning must be accomplished and finally the motive underlying the message or emotional tone deciphered. In expressive language an even more intricate network is involved, but first let us consider receptive language in greater detail.

In receptive language, the first step is the decoding or isolation of phonemes. This occurs in the second zone of the secondary functional unit, specifically in the second zone of the auditory (temporal) cortex. Here the precise or concrete understanding of the meaning of the words is accomplished. Also, possibly via connections to other associated areas (for example, visual), other impressions may be evoked by a visual image. Here, retention of all critical elements of the spoken language occurs. Next, the most significant elements of the language are decoded. Possibly for simple sentences and phrases this is not necessary, but certainly in complex sentences (especially abstract ones, or sentences where an underlying motive or emotional tone is involved), the tertiary functional unit is necessary to verify the just-received information and to initiate a planned response. Thus, concrete reception of the spoken sentence can occur through the primary and secondary unit, but more abstract language reception involves the tertiary unit.

Expressive language has somewhat different pathways but is similar in that for more complex or abstract speech, higher centers are involved. For example, in simple repetitive or perseverative speech there is little third functional unit input. However, in the production of spontaneous speech, especially spontaneous narrative speech (specifically if spontaneous gesturing or expressions are involved), the third functional unit is critical. Here a plan or action originates and is expressed via speech and other modalities. In translating the plan into action, internal language is necessary and it is also necessary to ensure a linear flow of the verbal response.

There are many more aspects to the reception and production of language; but from the above discussion, it can be seen that all three functional units are involved in understanding and production of language but the third functional unit is critical in spontaneous and complex language understanding and production.

LACK OF CEREBRAL DOMINANCE

The young child's brain is pliable to the extent that if a local lesion occurs in one hemisphere—say, in the dominant hemisphere—the non-dominant cerebral hemisphere would take over its function. However, if for some reason neither hemisphere showed dominance, could this produce the autistic syndrome?

This is the question asked by some researchers. It appears plausible that such a situation exists in view of the fact that certain autistic children do not show the usual differences in EEG (electroencephalograms) when comparisons are made over the recordings of the right and left hemispheres (Tanguay 1976). In normal brain function, progressive lateralization of function is present in the higher cortical zones. Beginning with the second zone of the secondary functional unit (the zone involved in association and coding) and also in the zones of the tertiary functioning unit, a progressive dominance of the left hemisphere is found. This is a unique finding in man and not present in other animals. This left cerebral dominance is responsible for right-handedness and is also the hemisphere involved in speech. It may thus be that if no cerebral dominance was present, speech would not develop. However, some researchers feel that there is a gradation of dominance in normal individuals, with some individuals showing very slight dominance, yet apparently without overt abnormalities (Luria 1973). However, even if a lack of cerebral dominance is not in itself the critical impairment, it could be a result of another impairment. The possibility of several of these defects coexisting will be discussed below.

In the above discussion, the possible mechanisms in producing autism were deliberately compared to normal brain function for two reasons. First, of course, the aim was to explain the theories against some framework so that each theory could be simplified and better explained. Secondly, however, the aim was to show how each of these theories has merit and yet need not be seen as "the answer." When viewed from the perspective of normal brain functioning, it is obvious that these theories are not mutually exclusive. Instead, the complexity of brain functioning makes it likely that problems in one area will affect other functional areas.

It is quite possible that one or two or even all these theories are correct. That is, there are defects in multiple areas, or rather defects in multiple areas arise as a result of one primary defect. For example, if a defect arises in the primary functional area, the screening of the initial sensory impulse will be affected as well as the cortical tone. In addition, *all* higher cortical areas may be affected. This is because in young children, where the zones are still developing, each successive area of normal growth is dependent on the development and normal functioning of the preceding functional area. The immature brain can readily take over functions of localized small lesions—for example, with a brain abscess—but such taking over of functions does not occur for entire zones. Sometimes this interaction of zones in young children has been termed as running "from below upwards"; that is, intact lower zones are essential for normal functioning higher zones. (Conversely, in adults, if a lesion occurs in a lower functional unit the higher functional unit can usually take over some of the function. In other words, the relationship of the zones is "from above downward.") Thus in children, a defect in the primary functional unit will affect the development of both the secondary and tertiary functional unit.

A defect in the secondary functional unit would affect the functioning of the primary by not providing adequate organization and coding of impulses received. Likewise, the same defect would affect the development of the tertiary unit according to the principle of hierarchical development as described for children. A tertiary unit's defect would of course influence all lower units as active regulation (by inner language, for example), or active planning and verification would be defective.

Thus it is quite possible that the various theories of autism are compatible and represent multiple observations of the same process. It is also quite possible that autism is not one entity, but that the syndrome may arise as a result of different mechanisms. The only way to determine which defect (or defects) *must* be present for autism to develop is for each group of investigators to pursue their investigations in these various directions, verifying correct hypotheses and discarding incorrect ones.

In summary, though as yet no specific cause has been found for autism, much progress has been made in the area. Most researchers today view autism as a developmental defect caused by some organic central nervous system impairment. This impairment could arise as a result of a biochemical, genetic, or other abnormality. In fact, it is quite possible that a number of such causes could produce the same CNS defect (or defects), which in turn produce the cognitive problems characteristic of autism.

In reviewing the mechanisms by which such cognitive problems arise, it can be seen that different levels of the CNS could be involved. In each mechanism, however, the impairment prevents the child from perceiving the world around him and prevents him from relating to it appropriately. This relating—or lack of relating—is thus a secondary problem resulting from a more basic impairment.

From a philosophical standpoint, one could deliberate whether this organic problem is also a type of psychosis. Years ago—but certainly not in use these days—was a term "accidental psychosis." This term referred to those individuals who would develop a psychotic disorder regardless of the environmental circumstances, for example, toxic psychosis. If psychosis refers to a severe impairment of both adaptation and perception of reality, then autism is a type of psychosis, but perhaps to be accurate autism should be called an "accidental psychosis."

4

OVERVIEW OF THERAPIES

A VARIETY of different therapeutic methods has been used with autistic children. The current trend is to use educational methods, since a structured skill development approach works best with these children. Details of educational approaches will be discussed in later chapters; in this chapter, therapeutic approaches used in clinics will be considered. We shall review the types of settings available and provide some suggestions as to how existing community resources can be utilized to develop a comprehensive program for an autistic child.

Before considering the controversies of various therapeutic methods, a more general controversy should be mentioned. Occasionally, seemingly unnecessarily, arguments have arisen as to where emphasis should be placed in working with autistic children—in the area of treating immediate problems or in searching for an etiology and prevention. From a historical perspective, a time-tested approach to any illness or disturbance has been to treat the symptoms while searching for a cause. This does not mean that every practitioner must engage in research or that every researcher must provide a treatment program. Rather, this means that the total efforts in the field of autism must be directed at providing therapy to deal with immediate problems *and* must explore more global approaches aimed at causality. To assume that if a cause is found, it will be untreatable is as much a disservice to present (and future) autistic children as saying that autistic children's behavior problems are unmodifiable or autistic children are untestable. Some workers have stated that there is a danger in emphasizing causes (such as genetic) which may seem unremediable. In response to this argument, it should be noted that with the current progress being made in genetic engineering (DNA research), it may be possible to change abnormal genes in the years ahead. Even more important, if autism is proven to be genetic in origin, then in some cases, with proper genetic counseling, parents can decide if they want to take the risk of having an autistic child. This discussion is not aimed at suggesting autism is genetic; in fact, as discussed in the etiology section, there is *little* evidence to suggest this. Rather, this discussion aims to stress the view that the search for a cause or causes of autism and the eventual development of a specific treatment plan is just as important as focusing on immediate problems.

Unfortunately, specific programs are still to be developed in the future. Currently, the types of therapies used are either aimed at target symptoms and promoting adaptive growth, or the therapy employed is a direct result of the therapist's theoretical stance of what may be the cause of autism. These forms of therapy can be divided into four groups: (1) therapy related to intrapsychic aspects; (2) therapy related to biochemical aspects; (3) therapy related to behavior modification; and (4) therapy using parents as therapists.

INTRAPSYCHIC ASPECTS

A number of earlier theories of autism revolved around the concept of environmental causality. Although only a few people adhere to this idea today, a sizable number of workers still feel that while the autistic child may be handicapped from birth, in addition, the environment does not meet his special needs. Therapy based on such a theoretical concept does not represent the major thrust of current work with autistic children, and the authors of this book do not subscribe to this theoretical orientation. However, for the sake of completeness, we shall look at brief examples of therapy based on the above principle.

Probably most prominent of the group stressing environmental causes is Bettelheim, who views autism as a withdrawal from a rejecting and frustrating world into a position of anger. The autistic child is not unable to relate to others; rather, underneath this façade of emptiness is anger and hate. Bettelheim's emphasis in therapy is a complete change of milieu with individualized therapy. He advocates (1967, 1974) inpatient settings like his Orthogenic School in Chicago, where young, totally dedicated staff are available on almost a constant basis to provide support, reassurance, and play therapy to aid the autistic child in giving up his withdrawal. This orientation is analytic and based on the idea that once the autistic child's underlying mechanisms are uncovered and worked through, and he can relate to his counselor in a normal fashion (show love and ambivalence), then improvement in other areas will follow.

Ward is a representative of the group who feels autism results when an innately vulnerable child is in an environment which cannot meet that child's special needs. Ward advocates the use of structural therapy for these children. This type of therapy is based on an approach used by Des Lauriers in the treatment of schizophrenic adolescents and is aimed at stimulating development of deficient ego processes. In this therapy, the child's stereotypic behavior is interrupted and the anger and anxiety resulting from this interruption is directed at the therapist, who then promotes constructive play, recognition of body parts, various new experiences, and language development. "This treatment approach postulates that the early infantile autistic child must be diverted from the 'dead end' of his behavioral ego level of functioning, stimulated and aided in the development of body ego, and finally assisted in developing age-appropriate object-relations" (Ward 1976).

These are only two examples of intrapsychic approaches; a number of other variations could be cited. Generally, however, all these approaches emphasize establishing a relationship with a therapist and, secondly, helping the autistic child either resolve intrapsychic conflicts or promote growth in an area of arrested psychic development.

Though a number of investigators using such approaches have reported favorable results, other investigators reviewing the general literature in this area have been more critical and feel that the insight-producing type of psychotherapy has not proven effective (Rutter 1967; Bartak and Rutter 1971).

BIOCHEMICAL ASPECTS

This general approach to intervention can be divided into two groups. In one group, the agent used is aimed at improving the general condition of the autistic child. In the second group, a drug is used as a therapeutic measure aimed at specific target symptoms.

Megavitamin Theory

Linus Pauling (1973) has suggested that an important means of therapy for psychiatric patients is orthomolecular therapy, which he defined as "treatment of mental disease by the provision of the optimum molecular environment for the mind [brain] especially the optimum concentration of substances normally present in the human body". Pauling felt that the brain is especially dependent upon chemical reactions and that mental illness frequently is due to abnormal chemical reaction rates. These chemical reaction rates are determined by "genetic constitution and diet, and by abnormal molecular concentrations of essential substances." As this need may be a local brain phenomena, the deficiency may not be evident in other parts of the body. Thus, the person may need more of essential substances in order to have normal mental functioning, but clinically or on laboratory tests no evidence of deficiency is seen. Some of these essential substances are certain vitamins—the B-complex (B_1, B_3, B_6, and B_{12}), biotin, folic acid, and ascorbic acid—as well as essential amino acids and essential fatty acids. Pauling theorized that large doses of vitamins were at times necessary to change reaction rates of enzymes and thus recommended megavitamin therapy for psychiatric conditions.

According to the above theory, Rimland has advocated the use of water-soluble vitamins in large doses in autistic children. Based on his experience and numerous reports by parents, he feels the results are often positive. A variety of severely disturbed children were examined in Rimland's study. However, he felt the autistic group of children showed the greatest improvement. Unfortunately, research in this area is inconclusive. Most studies are based on improvement being decided on purely clinical judgment, and very few of such studies control for possible bias.

In a double-blind study Rimland *et al.* (1978) found that when B_6 (pyridoxine) was withdrawn from 16 autistic-type children who had previously received the vitamin, deterioration occurred in the children's behavior. However, the authors caution that in this study there were many uncontrolled variables; even the apparent regression when the B_6 was withdrawn could be a sign of pyridoxine addiction. The authors concluded that vitamin therapy is of potential value and further investigation is warranted.

Generally this same sentiment is expressed by other persons working in the area of megavitamin therapy—there may be positive effects in some autistic children but much more investigation is necessary.

Levodopa (L-dopa)

As was mentioned in the section on etiology, one of the theories of the biochemical abnormalities in autism postulates abnormal levels of the neurotransmitter seratonin. Generally this area has many methodological problems, but since some autistic children have high blood levels of seratonin, researchers wondered if a decrease would show clinical improvement. L-dopa is a naturally occurring substance in the body. Its concentration in the brain is decreased in Parkinson's disease, and its major use is in treating this condition. One of its effects is in decreasing brain seratonin. When this drug was used with a small group of autistic children, their blood levels of seratonin decreased but no significant clinical improvement was seen in the children (Ritvo *et al.* 1971). In using this drug with a mixed group of disturbed children, Campbell (1973) found improvement in the group in the area of decreasing social withdrawal and increasing affective responsiveness. Thus it appears this drug will need to be investigated further.

Hormones

Though various hormones have been used in treating severely disturbed children, the hormone that shows the most encouraging results with autistic youngsters is thyroid. Thyroid is an important hormone in the maturation of the central nervous system, and either hypothyroidism or hyperthyroidism can have negative effects on the developing brain. Several investigators have used T_3 (tri-iodothyronine) in autistic children who did not clinically demonstrate either hypo- or hyperthyroidism. The results were encouraging, with statistically significant improvement (Campbell 1973). The use of thyroid in treatment of autistic children is another type of medical management meriting further investigation.

From the above discussion it can be seen that several avenues are currently being explored in the medical treatment of autism. None of these are proven methods, and all should be considered experimental. Frequently, in discussing experimental drugs, the question arises, "Why not try it anyway?" The answer is that unfortunately at times after a drug or mode of therapy has been sufficiently tested, it is proven inadequate or even worse—it is discarded because even though some positive effects were found, the negative effects in the long run outweigh them. Furthermore, a therapeutic method may work for some patients but not for others. For example, electric convulsive therapy (ECT) was initially introduced as a method of treating schizophrenic patients, and once this was used extensively even with schizophrenic children. It is currently considered a very effective method in treating adult depression, but is rarely used in adult schizophrenics and virtually never used in children.

Another problem in using an experimental drug is in the actual monitoring of and precautions taken while undergoing therapy. In experimental conditions, careful attention is paid to all possible negative effects, and either these can be counteracted or the regimen discontinued. In clinical practice monitoring is never as thorough, and minor negative effects may not be recognized till they become serious problems. For example, recently there have been reports of vitamin C dependency developing in persons taking excess amounts of this vitamin. Whether or not this could lead to decreased natural resistance to infections in such persons is not known, but such a result is certainly possible. Thus, even a seemingly harmless substance may produce some negative effects which can be controlled only by careful supervision.

In the future it may be possible to identify subgroups of autism; with more careful experimental data and careful classification, it may be possible to identify which group of autistic children will be more prone to show a positive response to one or another mode of medical intervention. This is still quite a ways off, and till then it is more reasonable for those parents who are interested in exploring new approaches to become involved with a reputable research approach rather than experimenting on their own (or by trying to convince their local physician to try a new program). All research groups are experimental, but for that very reason safeguards are built into these programs which cannot be readily duplicated outside of such settings.

DRUG THERAPY FOR TARGET SYMPTOMS

Drug therapy generally should be viewed as an adjunct to other therapy and not as a therapy in itself. It should only be used if the parents and the physician agree that indeed the situation or the child's symptoms merit this type of intervention. In addition, it should only be undertaken if adequate medical monitoring is available and the child can be carefully supervised at home and at school so that any side effects, unexpected negative reactions, and overdosage can be quickly recognized (Paluszny 1977).

Generally, children show fewer side effects to drugs than adults. On the other hand, children show greater variability in appropriate dosage (that is, the dose cannot always be predicted by weight and age). Furthermore, on general principles, using a drug in a growing organism and particularly in an autistic child who cannot communicate any physical discomfort related to the drug (such as dryness of the mouth or dizziness) merits careful consideration to determine if drug therapy is necessary. As Reiser (1963) stated, "Drugs that modify motor activity, anxiety, and emotional reactivity of the child further insulate him from his inner feelings and the outer world and may obliterate important cues that therapist and parents need."

Withdrawn Behavior

There appears to be no truly effective drug to combat the withdrawn, isolated behavior so often seen in autistic children. Antidepressants have been tried for this purpose, but negative effects have frequently been greater than the benefits. In one study where the antidepressant imipramine (Tofranil) was used in young autistic and schizophrenic children, increase of psychotic behaviors and the onset of grand mal seizures prompted the researchers to state that this drug should not be used except in the most "retarded, mute and anergic children" (Campbell *et al.* 1971). These investigators speculated that this drug (like several other antidepressants) potentiate the effects of seratonin which, as already described, has been implicated in the etiology of autism.

Stimulants are also poor medications in this group. Dexedrine and Ritalin generally serve as stimulants in adults, but in children these drugs are used to control hyperactivity. In autistic children, these drugs are often ineffective or, even if hyperactivity and aggressiveness are controlled, increased withdrawal may be produced. Neither stimulants nor antidepressants are generally used with autistic children.

Aggressive Behavior

Usually the major tranquilizers are used with autistic children for control of aggressive behavior which is either insufficiently controlled by other means or appears to be a severe interference in the child's learning and adaptive ability. The drugs most often used are Thorazine, Mellaril, Stelazine, and Prolixin. Though there are many individual variations, Stelazine and Prolixin may be more effective in the young autistic child. Stelazine in particular is a more potent drug, but one which has less sedative effects in young children. It was shown to be less likely to produce drowsiness and other side effects in the preschool age group. Thorazine and Mellaril, in contrast, are effective in older autistic children. Mellaril has been reported to be useful in control of rocking and other stereotypic behavior.

Lithium, though generally not used in autistic children, was used in an experimental group where the children's aggressive behavior was extremely difficult to control and unresponsive to other drug therapy. Though most of the children did not improve, one child completely stopped his self-mutilating behavior (Campbell *et al.* 1972). Lithium may be one of these drugs important in future explorations, but currently it is not a drug generally used with autistic children.

Epilepsy

As mentioned earlier, epilepsy occurs rather frequently in autistic children. Seizures may become apparent when the autistic child grows older (as during adolescence), or it may be prominent even in the early years. In either case, the seizures should be controlled if at all possible. Phenobarbital is one of the drugs commonly used as part of a regimen for convulsive disorders. Since phenobarbital frequently tends to increase hyperactivity and aggressiveness, this drug should be avoided, if possible, in the treatment of aggressive autistic epileptic children, and other anticonvulsants should be tried first.

Sleep Disturbances

Sleep problems—difficulty in going to bed and falling asleep or waking during the night—may cause a severe problem in the home of an autistic child. Medication may be used occasionally if other methods in controlling this difficulty have failed. Benadryl is basically an antihistamine, but because there are few side effects it is frequently used for its sedative properties in pediatric practice. This drug works especially well in young children and may be useful in nighttime sedation of the autistic child. Older autistic children usually respond well to chloral hydrate for nighttime sedation.

As can be seen from the above discussion, medication in the autistic child has very limited value. Drugs are used for target symptoms—primarily aggressive or self-mutilating behavior—and nighttime sedation. Even in these instances, however, other approaches should be tried first, and drug therapy should be used only as part of a total therapeutic program. Medication should always be carefully supervised through behavior observation, physical exams, and pertinent laboratory analyses, and the drug should be modified or terminated if there are side effects or lack of the desired response.

BEHAVIOR MODIFICATION

Behavior modification is currently the major therapeutic approach used with autistic children. This type of therapy has been compared to play therapy (Ney *et al.* 1971) and uncovering therapy (Bartak and Rutter 1971), and it seems to be more effective with autistic children. Since we shall examine this method in greater detail in Chapter 6, the discussion here is broad and introductory.

Behavior modification is based on learning theory, and it focuses the child's disturbance on external circumstances. The actual cause of the child's condition is unimportant. Rather, the child's behavior is viewed as a response to external stimuli. Treatment is not aimed at discovering the reason the autistic child does not speak or play; it is aimed at teaching him how to perform these functions.

The following steps are used in this method of therapy: (1) the behavioral therapist must first define the symptoms to be modified—either a behavior that is to be eliminated or one that is to be produced. (2) Next, the cues or stimuli which produce the behavior are identified. (3) A plan for therapy is mapped out. (4) Through the use of positive and/or negative reinforcement, in planned steps, the therapist moves the child's responses toward the behavior desired.

In defining the symptoms to be modified, priorities must be established. First, one must select the most critical symptoms to be modified. For example, in the long run the child's language ability may be judged to be most important for development of various skills, but if the child shows severe aggressive outbursts or self-mutilating behavior, these behaviors would be of top priority. After behaviors dangerous to the child and/or to others are eliminated, then the focus can be shifted to promoting various developmental skills such as language, toileting, or self-feeding.

After establishing a hierarchy of target symptoms or areas of skills to be developed, the therapist observes the child in an effort to determine cues or stimuli which produce the behavior. If such stimuli can be identified, efforts can be made to desensitize the child to the provoking stimuli or to modify or eliminate the stimuli. Conversely, in promoting desirable behaviors, the stimuli which elicit the behavior can be used as reinforcers. It is often difficult to see the provoking agent of some behaviors very readily, or the provocation is so slight and multiple in origin that the stimuli cannot be identified. For example, self-injury in autistic children may occur when the child is frustrated for a variety of reasons. In addition, some workers feel this behavior may also occur as an attention-getting device or even as a form of self-stimulation. Thus, frequently the stimuli eliciting this behavior are not identifiable, and behavior modification must be focused on the behavior only, rather than modifying both behavior and stimulus.

With self-injury as with other undesirable behaviors, one would generally attempt to eradicate the behavior using first the most positive and least noxious approach. The following descriptions of various procedures to eliminate an undesirable behavior represents such a scheme. However, it should be noted that this is primarily a description of various approaches, and not meant as a cookbook prescription of how behavior modification should be used. In the actual practice of behavior modification, careful notations must be kept on behavior improvement, and each approach must be tried numerous times before deciding that is does not work. Probably the major cause of failure of a behavior modification program is that the method was not used long or consistently enough.

Possibly the most positive approach in trying to eliminate a negative behavior is to reinforce the child for a different, positive behavior. Theoretically, then, as the positive behavior becomes more frequent, the negative will be less frequent. The child who is self-abusive can be reinforced for behavior that is not self-abusive. Such a child could be reinforced for screaming or expressing his aggression directly at some object other than himself. Finding such ways may call for much ingenuity and persistence. An interesting example of this is described by Carr (1976). A partially blind child persistently poked her fingers in her eyes. To stop this behavior an ingenious method was used to provide a competing stimulus. A recording was made of sounds the child especially enjoyed. Then, in order to play the recording, the child had to press two switches using both hands. However, this girl soon learned to press the switches with her elbows and still gouge her eyes with her fingers. The switches had to be altered so that only fingertips could be used to press them. The child thus was reinforced (by the sounds of the recording) for acceptable behavior.

Another behavior modification technique is based on the observation that children who show severe negative problems usually elicit much attention from those around them. Thus, in effect, the child is being reinforced for negative behavior. It is argued that if attention is withdrawn, then the behavior may cease. This may work with some children, but frequently it is virtually impossible to ask a child's parents and staff to do nothing while a youngster proceeds to mutilate himself. In one study (Bucher and Lovaas 1968), such an approach was effective in eliminating a child's head-banging, but not till the youngster had hit his head 10,000 times. The same authors elected not to try another child on a similar behavioral extinction procedure, for fear that the child could kill herself in the process. Obviously, extinction procedures used in severely self-abusive children must be used very cautiously and cannot be used with all such children.

A variety of punishment procedures have been used as negative reinforcers in behavior modification therapy. These have varied from deprivation of food, affection, or other "time out" procedures, to various restraining procedures, to more active aversive stimuli such as slapping, shaking, or electric shock. The more aversive a procedure is, the more caution must be taken. Severe aversive procedures should not be undertaken except in severe self-abuse or extreme aggression toward others. Even with less drastic measures, using aversive therapy must be carefully considered and not undertaken unless the parents, as well as various professionals working with the child, agree to this method of treatment. Many staff working with handicapped or disturbed children enter such professions because of their deep concern, and may not only be opposed to using aversive therapy but will do it inconsistently and with such reluctance that the method is bound to fail. The same is true for most parents. On the opposite side, the possibility of abuse of such methods is always present. In fact, abuse is probably more likely with the less severe aversive methods, since caution is greater with the more extreme punitive methods but with less drastic methods more errors are possible. For example, electric shock is not likely to be used except to eliminate severe aggressive problems and self-mutilation. This procedure is going to be used only by experts or at least under strict supervision. Yet slapping, shaking, or other forms of physical punishment may be used by parents, teachers, or people with little experience and minimal training.

If used properly, with due caution, aversive procedures can be useful when positive reinforcement has not been effective. This is particularly true in the more severely impaired retarded autistic child. The types of punishment procedures used can be divided into two groups. One group can be viewed as deprivation or removal of a positive reinforcer, and the second group consists of presentation of an aversive stimuli. The removal of a positive reinforcer can take different forms, but must be adjusted to the situation. For example, with a child who shows inappropriate behavior while eating (food-throwing, smearing), the food may be removed. Removal from a situation or time-out procedures may also be effective. Such procedures may include both removal from a situation and also negative reinforcement. For example, Hamilton et al. (1967) describe how a girl who frequently broke windows with her head was treated by a time-out procedure. The child was initially confined to bed, except for eating, bathing, toileting, and exercise. Later, when she was allowed up and around, she was returned to bed immediately after she broke a window. When this behavior ceased, the same procedure was used successfully in getting the girl to stop self-abuse and clothes-tearing.

Most of the time out, removal of positive reinforcers, or deprivation procedures are contingent on the undesirable behavior, that is, the procedure is instituted only following the negative behavior. Effective use of noncontingent time out has also been reported. Jones (1974) described the use of social isolation as a method of eliminating self-abuse in a 9-year-old child who previously had various unsuccessful aversive therapy (even electric shock). With careful control, the child had her restraints removed and was placed in an 8' x 10' isolation room equipped with a one-way mirror and a supply of toys for two-hour sessions twice daily. Initially the child showed much self-abuse in isolation, but this decreased, and eventually self-abuse outside of the isolation room was virtually eliminated. The total procedure took several months; then a year later self-abuse returned but was again eliminated in a similar manner.

Primary aversive stimulation contingent on self-abuse, aggressive outbursts, or other behavior dangerous to self or others has been used with a variety of children including autistic children. These types of procedures generally cause the most controversy and should be used only with the cautions stated earlier. However, in some cases such methods have proved to be very useful (Gardner 1970). Possibly the most controversial of these procedures has been the use of electric shock. Usually the shock is delivered by a hand-held inductorium, which delivers a painful shock but which is not strong enough to cause convulsions, loss of consciousness, or tissue damage. In reviewing the side effects of shock, it appears there are very few negative side effects except for a development of fears of the shock apparatus or of the therapist. Occasionally an increase in other behaviors have been reported, for example, an overall decrease in happiness or contentment (Lickstein and Schreibman 1976). Most researchers using shock with autistic children have reported positive results in that the target behavior was eliminated and no severe aftereffects were noted. However, in some cases the targeted inappropriate behavior recurred at a later time. Thus, shock may be effective in crisis situations to control a particularly dangerous behavior, but this does not appear to be a useful long-range treatment technique. The major thrust of therapy with autistic children must be in the area of building new skills. Eliminating negative reactions is only a first step in such a process.

In promoting positive development, systematic reinforcement of various skills has been used with autistic children. These skills have varied from simple attending behavior to establishing of self-care (such as toileting or self-feeding), to establishing complex abilities like language acquisition. In promoting a simple behavior, such as attending, the child can be reinforced by food or other methods simply each time eye contact is made. In establishing reinforcement for more complex behaviors, however, the behavior must be broken down into stages; each stage represents an individual unit for which the child is reinforced. After mastering one unit, the child moves on to the next stage. At first, reinforcement is presented in large quantities immediately after the desired response. Later, gradually, the reinforcement is decreased both in amount and frequency. In many programs tangible reinforcement is eventually replaced by nontangible reinforcers such as praise.

Often an aversive procedure will be used in addition to a positive reinforcer, but in each case a careful plan of skill building must be present if developmental tasks are to be successful. A good example of how a program can be built by initially decreasing negative behavior, then promoting attending and skill development, is the language program as implemented by Lovaas (1977). Since this program will be described later, it is only mentioned here as an example.

In summary, behavior modification is currently the basis for much therapeutic work with autistic children. Therapists should use positive reinforcement wherever possible, but negative reinforcement—deprivation of positive stimuli or using aversive stimuli—can be a useful method, especially in eliminating behaviors which prevent more constructive work with a child. Operant conditioning is frequently implemented in the classroom setting, and this will be discussed in greater detail later.

PARENTS AS THERAPISTS

In considering the autistic child's parents, it is difficult to separate what constitutes the parent/child relationship and what constitutes "therapy." For example, when a parent interrupts his or her autistic child's stereotypic play in order to hug the child, is this therapy or normal parent/child interaction? There is some overlap between these two types of interactions. This is of course true of all parent-child interactions; for example, the parent of a normal child who demonstrates looking both ways before crossing a street is acting as "a teacher." Certainly the role of parents encompasses many such roles. These various roles, as well as some general problems of living with an autistic child, are discussed in Chapter 7. In this section we shall consider only formal therapy carried out by parents. However, it is wise to remember that many other aspects of the parent-child interaction are therapeutic.

Several studies have appeared on developing home-based programs which use parents as therapists. Although different names have been used for such a program—Social Exchange (Kozloff 1973), Developmental Therapy (Schopler and Reichler 1971), and Home Based Program (Howlin et al. 1973)—most are based on principles of behavior modification. There are individual variations in these programs, but there are also many similarities. Typically, a thorough evaluation is made of the child's abilities and deficiencies. Parents' perceptions of the child are determined by interviews, questionnaires, and direct observation. The parents are trained in various ways—by observation of professionals with explanations of techniques, by direct participation in the training process, and eventually by weekly follow-up visits with the training personnel. In most of these programs, treatment sessions are done by the parent on a daily basis. The focus of therapy is generally on decreasing inappropriate behaviors and promoting skill development.

Keeping in mind the above-mentioned general comments of similarities in these programs, it is useful briefly to take a closer look at each program's actual implementation. The reader should consult particular works for more specific information.

Social Exchange Therapy

For the purpose of therapy, Kozloff (1973) describes autism as a set of behaviors which can be modified. The behavior is an exchange in which the autistic child and his parents participate. Exchanges can be initiated or reciprocated. The parent initiates an exchange by an "exchange signal"—by a directive ("Make your bed") or by setting up a contract ("when you make your bed, you can go out and play"). In each case the parent anticipates compliance, and the parents are encouraged to express expectations in such forms. The parent could, however, initiate an exchange by asking, "Could you make your bed?" This is a question, and it offers the child a choice of complying or not complying; for this reason, parents are taught not to use this form of an exchange.

After the parent has made the request, the child reciprocates by either complying with the request or not complying. The parent then promptly reciprocates by rewarding the behavior (with either tangible reinforcement—food or toys—or nontangibles such as praise or a hug). If the child did not comply, then the parent must be careful not to reinforce the behavior by negative attention. Instead, the parent can reciprocate in a negative manner by ignoring the child, or providing time out (isolating the child). The parent could also punish the child by spanking or taking away something the child values.

Parents are initially taught such approaches with observation and participation in the clinic. Later, the program moves to the home. A room with little distraction is selected in the home, and sessions are usually conducted at the same time each day. The parent sits close to the child and, using food or other reinforcers, takes a step-by-step approach to teach the child various skills. Some of the areas specifically worked on are: eye contact; developing constructive behavior (teaching the child play and chore skills through learning manipulation of objects); motor imitation; and speech therapy. Each of these objectives is broken down into small units in which a step-by-step approach is followed for implementation. Furthermore, these stages are broken down in such a way that much of the behavior learned during the structured sessions can be used and appropriately reinforced during the remainder of the day.

Developmental Therapy

Schopler and Reichler's (1971a) program uses many of the general principles mentioned earlier as common to programs utilizing parent-therapists. There is an initial observation/training period, and thereafter the therapy done at home is monitored. In addition to showing the professional therapist how the parent is working at home during the structured sessions, the parents meet at a separate time to discuss daily problem areas not immediately related to the structured sessions such as sleep disturbances and toileting.

The structured sessions are concerned with four areas:

HUMAN RELATEDNESS

The child is encouraged to relate to the adult and is not allowed to avoid such interaction. Self-stimulation, withdrawal, walking away, etc., are prevented, while initial contact is reinforced by food or other means.

COMPETENCE MOTIVATION

Here, the aim is to help the child develop pleasure and interest in toys and educational materials. Exploration is encouraged, along with other skills necessary for play.

COGNITIVE FUNCTIONS

The major emphasis is on developing both receptive and expressive communication. This is adjusted to the individual child. One child may focus primarily on imitative behaviors, while another will be worked with in encouraging sounds or identifying objects by name. In still higher-functioning children, abstract concepts such as the difference between "up" and "down" are worked on.

PERCEPTUAL MOTOR FUNCTION

The child's awareness and coordination of his body is promoted by eye-hand coordination exercises and gross motor exercises. Again, individual variations are accounted for. One child may need passive manipulation of his limbs to develop body awareness and coordination, while another child may learn discrimination of shapes and then progress to learning letters.

In evaluating progress Schopler and Reichler generally found that autistic children did better in structured situations. However, the degree of structure necessary was related to the child's level of functioning. The lower-level autistic child needed more structure, while the higher-level autistic child managed with less. It appeared that more structure was necessary in the initial learning stage, and then, once a skill was mastered, less structure was needed in order to practice the learned skills. Thus, these workers feel rigid operant conditioning is not always the best approach.

Home-Based Approach

Although this approach is in many ways similar to the others, Howlin et al. (1973) offer a very careful description of behaviors to be encouraged or discouraged as well as the actual procedure and time required to accomplish the results. The overall program—in terms of initial assessment, training for parents, and monitoring—is similar to the other programs, but the initial emphasis is on changing those behaviors the parents find most difficult to handle (such as ritualistic behaviors, toilet training, self-care skills, road safety, hyperactivity). Language remediation is also a major emphasis.

These investigators also point out some important problems in this type of approach. For example, marital problems or other family difficulties can significantly affect the usefulness of the parent-therapist. Although parents could learn specific ways of handling situations, generalizing from these to new situations (which would allow the parent-therapist to work independently without supervision) was frequently not successful. Thus, in addition to demonstrating techniques various types of counseling or support for the parents are often important.

In summary, therapy for autistic children is progressing, but it is still fraught with many problems and unanswered questions. Currently, behavior modification (at times used with medication) has been used effectively to decrease specific behavior problems. The development of new skills has been approached through various educational techniques (discussed in Chapter 6) and by parent training. Using parents as therapists is effective from the standpoint of helping the parent learn skills to manage the autistic child. This can also serve as a useful way of integrating a home and school program. However, one should not conclude that parents can take over the complete program for an autistic child, whose problems need the combined efforts of many specialists as well as parents and teachers.

TREATMENT SETTINGS

Perhaps one of the greatest problems with having an autistic child is in finding adequate services or treatment programs. It is typical of today's services that they are either inadequate or unwilling or unable to modify their programs to be of maximum benefit to the growth of the autistic child. We shall look at therapy conducted through mental health clinics, psychiatric facilities, and other institutions related to medical approaches. Remedial education programs, discussed in Chapters 5, 6, and 7, probably are the major therapeutic setting for autistic children today.

Most treatment programs can be implemented in either an outpatient or an inpatient setting. Some programs, however, are typically geared toward one or the other. In recent years, the day treatment approach has been frequently used for autistic children. This type of setting aims to provide the advantages of both inpatient and outpatient therapy while minimizing the disadvantages of either setting. The inpatient approach was most common in the 1940s and 50s. Later, outpatient and day treatment approaches evolved, and now inpatient therapy for autistic children is usually used only under certain circumstances.

Inpatient Therapy

Since the late 1960s conditions previously handled on an inpatient basis are more likely to be treated on an outpatient basis. This has been true of mental retardation and various psychological problems, and it is also true of autism. Part of this trend of treating autistic children on an outpatient basis is due to the general trend of deinstitutionalization and also better provision of services in the community. However, other factors are also important. In the 1950s and even in the 1960s the predominant theories of autism focused on the parents' being causative agents. In order to rectify this condition, it was thus necessary to remove the child from the home environment to a different milieu. As more research was done on autism, and it became increasingly clear that the autistic child's handicap is an organic problem, different approaches were tried. Currently, if inpatient therapy is indicated for an autistic child, special schools are used rather than inpatient psychiatric facilities. Such schools are reminiscent of boarding schools for normal children or special training schools for retarded children. These facilities do not emphasize psychotherapy but rather teaching through a variety of educational approaches.

The psychiatric hospital approach is still used with autistic children, but usually this is short-term. An autistic child is usually admitted into such a setting for three reasons. First, the autistic child may be admitted as an inpatient for diagnostic studies and to initiate treatment. This may be the beginning of a behavior modification program or another type of program which will be implemented later on an outpatient basis. In the initial inpatient phase, baselines are established in the child's behavior. This initial phase is also important in developing a working relationship between parents, staff, and child. Secondly, an autistic child may be admitted to a psychiatric facility for respite care. Not infrequently, managing an autistic child at home becomes an almost impossible task for parents. For the purpose of taking family vacations or perhaps during times of crisis, some facilities will accept autistic children for several days up to several weeks. The third, and perhaps at times the most frustrating and complicated, type of admission occurs when the child either is not responding to outpatient or day care treatment or even appears to be getting worse. Occasionally, increased withdrawal and isolation as well as a regression in previously achieved skills may be the reason for initiating a hospitalization. Most often, however, such a suggestion is made when the autistic child shows increasing aggressive behavior. Such a child may bite, scratch, or hit at unpredictable times, seemingly without provocation. Usually an outpatient evaluation is requested, and the outcome of the evaluation may be a recommendation for inpatient therapy. Unfortunately, in most states inpatient units and outpatient clinics work separately, and frequently the parents and autistic child get caught in the middle of bureaucratic requirements. Since this has happened to many parents of autistic children, it may be useful to review some of the problems encountered when inpatient therapy is recommended for an autistic child who is not responding to outpatient therapy.

Problems immediately arise in trying to get a child admitted. The professionals making the recommendation usually must submit lengthy evaluations telling why they believe inpatient treatment is required. Despite this information, most facilities will also require a repeat evaluation in their own facility prior to admission. The parents must also meet certain criteria—live within the facility's "catchment area," be willing to be involved in therapy themselves, etc. Most often, the autistic child himself must meet certain criteria. The child's level of functioning is carefully evaluated, and frequently the question of retardation is raised. Sometimes the suggestion is made that the child would be more suitably placed in a facility for retarded children. The child's level of aggressiveness is often considered. If the child is too aggressive, and the facility's staff feel they have insufficient personnel to cope with this behavior, the child may be rejected. Another factor weighed in the decision to admit or not admit a child is the child's age. Usually, children under four or five years of age are not accepted for inpatient care.

After thinking of all these problems, one may readily feel that the inpatient facility's major aim is to find some reason to refuse admission. This, of course, is not true. In considering inpatient policies for admission, most of the time one can find good and just reasons for their existence. For example, the "catchment area" rule may be mandated not by the facility itself but by higher state units, such as the Department of Social Services or Mental Health. Funds are usually appropriated to a facility on a regional basis by such agencies. Furthermore, adhering to this policy ensures a uniform patient distribution. Screening the autistic child's parents is a routine procedure for all parents of prospective inpatients. It is necessary to determine if the parents will cooperate with the program. It is also necessary to acquaint the parents with the facility so that once the child is admitted, disillusioned or dissatisfied parents do not remove the child against medical advice.

Perhaps the most important criteria are those applied to the child. No child should be hospitalized unless it is necessary. The necessity for hospitalization may arise for many reasons, but the inpatient facility has the ultimate responsibility for this decision and thus cannot treat it lightly. Furthermore, many autistic children are also retarded. Facilities usually have an existing psychiatric program or a program for retarded children. Ideally, of course, programs for autistic children should provide services for both the higher functioning autistic child, as well as the retarded autistic child. In reality, such services are rarely found, especially on an inpatient setting. Thus, the hospital personnel must make a decision as to which existing facility comes closer to meeting the child's needs.

Aggressive behavior in a child is important with regard to adequate safety for other children, but, except in rare instances, exclusion or inclusion in a program is not determined on this basis. Age, on the other hand, may be a critical factor. Most facilities organize therapeutic programs not only according to the child's type of disturbance, but also according to his age. This is done to provide peer role models as well as to allow some uniform programming of activities. Most facilities have children involved in school type activities throughout a major portion of the day. If the child is too young for such programs, he must either remain on the ward just with the staff and with no planned program, or a special program must be provided just for him. Obviously, the first alternative (of the child being without a program) is detrimental to the child. The second alternative (of a new program being established) is a good alternative for the child but unfortunately not feasible for most facilities since establishing a new program for just one child is too costly and inefficient.

From the above discussion, it can be seen that admitting an autistic child to a psychiatric inpatient facility may present problems. There are also several major disadvantages to inpatient treatment for autistic children. Of most importance is the fact that psychiatric facilities are aimed at providing psychotherapy. Most workers in the area of autism do not feel this is an appropriate approach. In the mid-1960s, when it was thought that early life experiences leading to frustration, hostility, and withdrawal were critical in the development of the autistic syndrome, it seemed appropriate to remove the child from the home and use psychotherapy in treating autism. Now, however, since more and more evidence points to a perceptual or cognitive defect, remedial education approaches, speech therapy, and behavior modification are more effective routes of reaching the autistic child. Furthermore, the current trends in therapy place much responsibility on parents. The parents frequently become lay therapists under the supervision of a professional therapist. Removing the child from his home for long periods of time can interfere with the therapeutic aspect of the parent-child interaction as well as the usual aspects of that relationship.

As already mentioned, the current trend is to hospitalize autistic children *only* for brief periods. This can be done to initiate a new program, to provide respite care, or to assess why a child is regressing or not making progress. Inpatient psychotherapy can be viewed as a back-up service which provides support when necessary but is not the major provider of therapy for autistic children.

Outpatient Therapy

Although a variety of outpatient facilities are available in most communities, few of them provide adequate programs for autistic children. Communities may have university centers or psychiatric clinics as part of a general hospital or an outpatient service as part of a psychiatric hospital. Community mental health clinics, child guidance clinics, and private practitioners (psychiatrists, psychologists, and social workers) provide services to many children and their families. Unfortunately, the autistic child with his special needs is frequently not provided with suitable services. Partly this is due to the professionals' feeling of futility—a feeling that the usual services provided to a child and his family on an outpatient basis will be a "drop in the bucket" when it comes to the autistic child. This feeling is difficult to dispel, because there is much truth in it; the *usual* outpatient services are a drop in the bucket. If the only therapy done with an autistic child is a once-a-week session in an outpatient clinic, this is inadequate. It does not even matter what the emphasis of the session is—whether it is aimed at establishing a relationship, behavior modification, or another form of therapy—once a week is plainly insufficient. About the only type of therapy feasible on a once-a-week basis for an autistic child would be the monitoring of medication.

If once-a-week therapy is inadequate, then what can be done in an outpatient clinic? Realistically, most clinics have so many demands for their time that it is impossible to see one child many times each week. The only solution to this problem appears to be a team approach, which will be discussed at the end of this chapter.

Another important function for the typical outpatient mental health clinic is to provide support for families. In the case of the autistic child, this may be in the form of locating appropriate community resources. This can mean finding and referring the child to an inpatient service (if for some reason inpatient is necessary), or helping the family with the referral to a live-in school for autistic children or some other facility. Occasionally, a member of the clinic's staff can act as spokesman for the child's family in the school placement. This can be particularly useful if the school feels little progress is being made and something more needs to be done. As an impartial professional, the outpatient social worker, psychologist, or psychiatrist can help the school reassess its program and the child's progress. This tactic is especially useful when the school and the parents disagree about the child's needs and how these are being met at the school.

Perhaps the most controversial type of support involves working with the parents. In the past, many clinics were highly influenced by the view that autism arises as a result of problems in early parent-child interaction. Parents were evaluated for possible signs of conscious or unconscious rejection of the child. Any personality deviation in the parents could be easily enlarged and judged as the "culprit" trait responsible for the child's pathology. It is not surprising that many parents turned away from this type of "help" and sought services through other sources. Now, in many instances, even if the parents of an autistic child feel the need for counseling either around their autistic child or related to another problem, understandably they experience much hesitancy in consulting an outpatient clinic. This is unfortunate, as most professionals can be of help in counseling parents in a variety of ways—for example, in helping them reach a reasonable compromise between commitment to the handicapped child and the many other obligations they have, or in helping them decide if the child should continue living at home, or most important, in helping the two parents reach agreement on these and other vital issues.

In working with the parents of an autistic child, an outpatient therapist may use the model followed by many clinics in working with parents who have a chronically handicapped child. In many such clinics, no attempt is made to correct the initial condition, but rather to prevent additional problems from developing and to give support and counsel to the parents as the child matures and different issues emerge. As already mentioned, the treatment of an autistic child cannot be effectively carried out on a once-a-week basis, but counseling—both to prevent additional problems, during crises, or at times when shifts or changes occur either in the autistic child or in the family situation—can be very helpful.

Day Treatment

The combination of school and therapy, implemented in one setting on a daily basis, is the ideal approach for helping many autistic children. This can be done in a special class, but it is more effective in a special unit. In a classroom the child is limited to that one area, and a consistent program cannot be maintained in the lunchroom or playground, where there is a mixing of children. A special unit which consists of special schooling with a therapeutic intent is probably best. In many parts of the country, day treatment programs are available through the school system, while in others such programs are run by mental health clinics or child guidance clinics. In either case, most of these programs provide a school program integrated with various other services. Some will have as part of the therapeutic team a speech therapist, an occupational therapist (or physical therapist), a social worker, a psychologist, and consulting psychiatrist or pediatrician. The typical day treatment unit operates on a five-days-a-week basis, with each child coming to the program five to six hours per day. A major emphasis during this time is on cognitive learning and also on learning more appropriate socially acceptable behaviors. For this purpose, a form of behavior modification technique is often used, emphasizing positive rather than negative reinforcement. Speech therapy is often used as part of the language training program, and occupational therapy is used to help in coordination, exploration of physical boundaries, and increasing awareness of one's body. Parents are often involved in such day treatment units, either as participants in a group whose members can share information, or—as is becoming more common now —as auxiliary therapists who can learn and implement techniques used at the day treatment center in their own homes.

Unfortunately, there are many areas of the country which do not have special day treatment units. Furthermore, some existing day treatment programs are not as effective as they should be. Either because of lack of resources, lack of training of personnel, or unwillingness for staff and parents to work together, some day care units experience fragmentation in the program, with consistency and structure giving way to haphazard implementation of therapeutic and educational techniques. Under such circumstances, the parents can feel particularly disappointed and frustrated. To have a long-sought program disintegrate, for whatever reason, can be the ultimate blow for parents who frequently have experienced too much pain already in seeking help for their autistic child. It should be remembered, however, that many programs for autistic children arose out of the parents' ability and willingness to pressure and cajole appropriate authorities to develop these programs; if existing programs do not meet their objectives, the same pressure can be used to improve the program. In effect, just as the professional should include parents in their work with the autistic child, the parents must continue to be involved with the program and be ready to use their influence if the program starts to deteriorate.

A MODEL

From the discussion on treatment methods and settings, it can be seen that the best therapeutic approach is one emphasizing close integration of services provided through parents, educators, and other professionals. The ideal model may be described in the following way: the autistic child is living at home, where his behavior and skill development are promoted by the parents. The parents are trained and monitored in their work by staff from a day treatment unit. In the day treatment unit, various professionals—psychologist, psychiatrist, speech therapist, and social worker—are available to work with the teacher in developing a school program. These same personnel are available to do periodic assessments and to help the parents in their role as parent-therapists. Additional services are available in the community for periodic physical exams and dental care. Likewise, crisis or short-term intervention is readily accessible in the form of an inpatient setting for respite care, and either a pediatrician or psychiatrist who will prescribe and monitor medication if this is necessary. Periodic evaluation of the total program and the child's progress is done routinely, and change is implemented when necessary.

Many (possibly most) communities do not have such programs, but most communities have the basic ingredients for organizing such units. For example, the following plan could be used.

Resources

Since autism is rare, there are few experts. Even if a person has had some experience in working with autistic children, this is usually in one disciplinary area. However, by sharing, expertise is quickly built up, perhaps by exchanging consultants from various disciplines and from various settings. Inservice training or sending several key people to established centers working with autistic children can be a start, to be built on later.

Organizing Existing Services

Typically, schools, guidance clinics, university or other research centers, and hospitals all work independent of one another. However, it is possible to unify these agencies and coordinate their work on one case. The research or university center can act as a pool of interdisciplinary consultants who make initial and periodic assessments and also help with programming for the autistic child. The school and guidance clinic personnel can work on a weekly basis with the parents to help them in developing the child's skills at home and in helping them to handle problem behavior appropriately. The guidance clinic can work with other community agencies to establish respite care as well as routine medical and dental services. In addition to frequent meetings with the guidance clinic, the school must maintain an even closer liaison with the parents, so that the home program and school program are not two separate programs but just different aspects of the same cohesive program.

Although this seems a tremendous amount of liaison, it becomes less difficult and more manageable if the same people for each agency are involved with several autistic children. Often the development of such an interagency team can be very useful not only in providing better services for the child and his family, but in providing support and practical suggestions through sharing of ideas for each of the team members.

5

EDUCATIONAL RESPONSIBILITY

James L. Paul

and

Rebecca Posante-Loro

AUTISM is one of the most complex psychoneurological problems of childhood. Until recently the knowledge base was very narrow. Research efforts focused on explaining the phenomenon and attempting to rationalize the manifestation within the existing theoretical frameworks of psychology. The well-known substantive nature-nurture debates between the genetic theorists and the psychoanalytically oriented theorists produced relatively little of clinical value in altering the prognosis of the disease. Given the intractability of the problem and the small number of children affected by it, clinical research efforts were limited in scope.

The development of a more credible base of knowledge about the nature and treatment of autism has, however, become more important in the 1970s. The primary reason for this is that the law now assures that every child shall be provided a free appropriate public education (P.L. 94-142, 1975). In order to fully implement that law, it is necessary to have administrative, social, and clinical educational concepts and practices which make the education of these children feasible.

Sarason and Gladwin (1959) pointed out the importance of understanding autism to the development of a science of psychology. At the present time, the development of relevant educational concepts and effective methods for teaching these children is important to the development of the philosophy and science of education.

In medical and psychological literature there has been an important change in the professional perspective on the nature of autism. Ritvo (1976) has characterized this as the change from using autism as an adjective, which characterizes a type of behavior, to using it as a noun indicating a disease entity. Ritvo describes autism as a physical disease, arguing that while the specific cause of neuroanatomical and biochemical pathology are unknown, systematic treatment has been developed for these children. This neurophysiopathological view of autism has released parents previously held hostage by psychoanalytic views which considered

93

the early nurturing by parents as central to explaining the emergence of autism (Bettelheim 1967). This new view has relieved parents of compounded guilt and also made parents available as essential resources in habilitation programs. The development and demonstration of parent training as a key feature of treatment programs such as Treatment and Education of Autistic and Related Communications Handicapped Children (TEACCH) and Regional Intervention Project (RIP) described in Chapter 6 has been one of the most significant developments in this field since the late 1960s. Two characteristics of these programs are especially important in redirecting treatment of children with autism: they have used parents as cotherapists or teachers, and they have focused their interventions on the present behavior and circumstances of the child and his living environments. In most of these programs there has been a strong interdisciplinary orientation.

Educational responsibility is based on several important changes that have taken place in understanding autism. These changes include the predominant view that autism is a neurophysiopathological condition, considering parents as allies in the treatment regimen, the development of behavioral methodologies, and the interdisciplinary orientation to the understanding and treatment of the problem.

EDUCATIONAL AND PHILOSOPHICAL CHANGES

During the last fifteen years the philosophy and practices of special education have changed dramatically. Two important aspects of that history are particularly important in understanding the present status of the philosophy and technical foundation for developing educational services for autistic children. First is the educational thought and practices with regard to children viewed as disturbed; second is the view of children as neurologically impaired. Each aspect has been productive and contributes to the emerging philosophy and practice of educating autistic children who have been viewed historically within each framework.

Emotionally Disturbed

Until the middle sixties, special education was primarily for the mentally retarded, the crippled, and those with sensory impairments. As a result of the Kennedy administration's efforts, together with the support of parent organizations, federal legislation increased the resources available for special education services for a larger group of handicapped children. Among those to receive substantial education services for the first time were the emotionally disturbed. Autism, at that time, was considered one of the most severe emotional disturbances.

The assumption of educational responsibility for emotionally disturbed children was, in its own right, a revolution in thinking about the proper domain of educational responsibility. Emotional disturbance has been the exclusive domain of the mental health system. Acquiring a psychiatric label was one way in which children who violated the behavioral norms of schools were excluded from school.

There were several important reasons for mixing psychological and educational concepts in order to understand autistic children and involve teachers in their treatment. One reason was the research into the mental health professional personnel available to work with these children. Albee's studies (1959) pointed out the futility of the mismatch between the scope of the problem and the professionals available. There were not enough trained people, and with the existing training practices there would never be enough child psychiatrists, child psychologists, and psychiatric social workers trained to implement traditional mental health services to meet the need. A new form of professional was needed to augment and expand the work of traditional mental health specialists.

Another reason was the lack of evidence that traditional clinical practices worked, especially with seriously disturbed children. The need for a public health model was further pointed out by the class bias of mental health practices as indicated by the classical New Haven study by Hollingshead and Redlich (1958).

It was in this context that the radical concept of teachers working with emotionally disturbed children was tested in the early sixties. These efforts were initially made by the National Institute of Mental Health through programs such as project ReEducation. The same programs that involved teachers more directly in working with these children involved the traditional mental health specialists in new roles as consultants to and trainers of those teachers.

In the middle sixties, training programs for teachers of emotionally disturbed children were developed in colleges and universities to staff the special programs being developed in schools. The most common program to emerge was the special class for the emotionally disturbed (Morse, Cutler, and Fink 1964). The psychoeducational perspective, a combination of clinical classroom concepts, was the prevailing view.

The autistic child did not, however, benefit substantially from this new movement in education. These children were still, for the most part, in institutions or at home. Even in institutions, educational services were viewed more as ancillary than primary.

Three criteria of the typical psychoeducational service in the mid to late sixties excluded autistic children. Children had to be able to benefit from the curriculum and relationships; autistic children were considered too severely disturbed. Many programs excluded children if there was an apparent organic base to the disorder, arguing that the process was irreversible and the primary problem, organicity, was outside the purview of education. The organic hypothesis was very prominent when autistic children were staffed for educational programs. A third criterion was that the children qualifying for services for the emotionally disturbed not be retarded. Given the problem of intellectual assessment of autistic children and the complexity of a differential diagnosis, these children were also excluded on this basis.

However, the adaptations of the educational system in the middle sixties to provide educational services for children with behavioral deficits form the headwaters of changes in philosophy and practices and administrative arrangements that ultimately came to support these children. Unlike education for the retarded, where the educational goals are reduced, or for the crippled and sensory impaired, where prosthetic devices circumvent the disability to allow the child to use the normal curriculum, the educational issues for the disturbed were different. Since the problem could not be mechanically or physically circumvented, and it could not be rationalized as an intellectual deficit, attention was necessarily turned to the affective and behavioral goals of education.

In the late sixties, the problem of disturbance was redefined in many educational settings. While the educational system had assumed more responsibility for disturbed children, the psychoeducational perspective employed had not proven very efficient or effective. Special classes for the emotionally disturbed were not as successful when compared with the educational benefits of regular classes (Rubin, Simson, and Betwee 1968). It was at this time that behavioral methodologies became available and were transferred from the laboratory setting to the classroom. The power and efficiency of the procedures were so impressive and the need was so great that behavior modification programs spread very rapidly.

Results of important studies such as those by Lovaas with autistic children (1965, 1966) raised the hope of more effective programming. While the researchers never advanced the view, there was a spirit of ultimate solution or cure by the more enthusiastic proponents of the operant procedures. This was not unlike the fantasy of the late 1800s, triggered by discoveries in topographical neurology, that a cure could be found for mental illness. That is, the hope for the potential of behavior modification, in the minds of many enthusiastic proponents during the late sixties, was similar to the hope for psychosurgery in the late 1800s.

Behavior modification procedures were effective in working with autistic children, but there continued to be a ceiling on achievement. In the early seventies therapists came to accept behavior modification as an additional powerful methodology to use in working with autistic children and not a solution to the many psychological problems involved in autism. Behavioral approaches were incorporated into structured educational curricula (Hewett-Engineered class 1968) and into a parent training program, RIP (Ora 1973).

Special education of emotionally disturbed children in the early seventies continued to be a very confused mixture of fragments of psychological, medical, sociological and educational theories. Rhodes and his colleagues at the University of Michigan studied the prevailing views of child variance to assist the field of Special Education, particularly in teacher training, in developing a more thoughtful and philosophically credible view of the phenomenon of variance in children (Rhodes and Tracy 1973). More recently Rhodes and Paul (1978) have reviewed the current theories and practices and the philosophical, scientific, and political bases for directions in the education of deviant children.

There continue to be basic philosophical differences between educational practices with these children. Few, however, focus exclusively on either psychodynamic or behavioral views as they did in the sixties. The more common view combines elements of different perspectives. One of the most promising paradigms is provided by the ecological perspective. This is not an independent theory, but rather an integrative framework which makes use of dynamic, behavioral, and sociological perspectives (Rhodes and Paul 1978). The basic principle of this view is that disturbance or deviation is a problem of negative adaptation, or a "bad fit" between the child and his environment. The child and the setting are disturbed by and disturbing to each other. The problem is not reducible to inadequacies in the child, the curriculum, or the setting. The problem is in the collection of the different interactive parts which do not work together in such a way that both individual and setting needs are met.

This basic view has important ethical implications as well as implications for educational program planning. An important ethical implication is that responsibility for behavior is shared. The programmatic implication is that planning must focus on the interaction, including the tolerance threshold of the setting as well as the behavioral deviation of the child. The setting is a powerful force in the control of behavior, and disturbance is not constant across settings. Many programs for the emotionally disturbed have used this basic view to rationalize the development of new role models, such as the liaison teachers, and to develop community service-integration models. Focusing on interaction has also helped take the "either-or" thinking out of educational placement, i.e., either a regular class or a special class; either an institution or a community. Many administrative arrangements, such as the resource room, and support roles, such as the crisis teacher, have been developed to work with children at specific points of difficulty rather than removing the child completely from his normal peer group.

With autistic children, whose behavior is so aberrant and whose psychopathology is so pervasive, much of the interaction is, indeed, understood in relation to their intractable habit patterns and inability to relate or use language. There are four relevant points here: (1) the emergence of the interactionist or ecological perspective in education in relation to providing educational services for behavior disordered children; (2) the quasisynthesis of theories of child variance; (3) the extent to which there exists a conceptual basis for the educational environment to examine its own impact on the interaction called "disturbed"; and (4) the development of new role models and alternative administrative arrangements. All of these are important in the developing philosophical basis and technical and administrative capacity of schools to provide relevant educational services for autistic children.

Neurology

Another important stream of educational activity which flowed from the political headwaters of the early sixties when educational responsibility was expanded to include children with different types of handicaps involved the education of learning disabled children. In the early to middle sixties these children were referred to as "brain injured," "brain damaged," "neurologically impaired," or any one of more than thirty other labels used by different professionals (Cruickshank and Paul 1971).

Prior to the early sixties, these children had received no special services. They had been misplaced in classes for the retarded or left in regular classrooms where they performed poorly and in many instances failed academically. The chronic failure of these children, frequently viewed as lazy or unmotivated, resulted in behavior problems and exclusion from school for many of them.

Much of the early research into the learning characteristics of children with suspected neurological impairments was done with the mentally retarded (Strauss and Lehtinen, Vol. I, 1947). While most retarded children were found to have learning characteristics that differed from their non-retarded chronological peers only in rate of learning, some of the retarded were found to have different learning characteristics. This group, approximately 15 percent, were suspected of having organic pathology involving the central nervous system. They were called "exogenously retarded." While the precise relationship between the neuropathology and the learning characteristics of these children was not determined, the psychopathology was well described. This served as the foundation for the work of many educators and psychologists investigating the manifestation of similar psychopathology in children with normal intelligence but with serious learning deficits. Cruickshank was one of the major advocates of this psychoneurological perspective and led the way in much of the investigation into the psychopathology of the intellectually normal, perceptually impaired group. He focused much of his work on the perceptual motor area and the resultant psychological consequences for the development of self-esteem. The direction of his investigations was to ascertain the learning deficits and to develop a curriculum to reduce or otherwise circumvent the psychopathology of these children and ultimately make them more amenable to the regular educational curriculum (Cruickshank et al. 1961; Cruickshank 1967, 1977). One of his major contributions has been and continues to be his very strong advocacy for an interdisciplinary perspective in understanding and teaching these children.

There were several important theoreticians who made important contributions in this area in the sixties including Kephart (1971), Barsch (1968), Gallagher (1960), Mykelbust (1964), Rappaport (1964), and Getman (1968). These are described in other literature (Cruickshank and Paul 1978). The important issue here is the nature and scope of this work in the early to mid-sixties which focused on the educational needs of children who were viewed as neurologically impaired.

Kirk (1962, 1971) and Bateman (1964) were particularly important theorists during this period whose work focused on intellectually normal children with serious learning problems. Their work centered more on language, and they were leaders in the move to direct attention away from the presumed neurological substrate of the problem. As a result of his address to the National Association for Children with Learning Disabilities in 1971, Kirk was perhaps most responsible for the term "learning disability" emerging as the term of choice. The selection of this term in the early seventies was important because of the philosophical shift implied. It is not necessary to deny the neurological component, and the possible etiological role of organicity, in order to shift the emphasis to learning behavior. The etiological questions continued to be extremely important, particularly in the ultimate development of effective preventive measures. Etiology and prevention are interdisciplinary research issues which challenge the efforts of many social and physical science areas. The formulation of a knowledge base on brain-behavior relationships, genetic factors, and microbial, nutritional, or social-environmental hazards to neural development are research frontiers already being explored. It is as exciting as it is essential. However, it is not (as once thought) a necessary precondition to programmatic research and development. There have been impressive gains in functional assessment (Flaharty 1976; Reichler and Schopler 1976; DeMyer *et al.* 1971) and in programmatic knowledge for teaching these children (Rutter and Sussenwein 1971; Kozloff 1972; Gallagher and Wiegerink 1976; Strain and Wiegerink 1975). The shift from a neurological (medical) to a learning (psychoeducational) orientation was accompanied by a shift from concern with how to teach these children, given the learning characteristics they manifest.

Most of the different social and physical sciences involved have had basic theoretical as well as applied clinical interests. The refocus in the late sixties, however, was productive in reducing some of the medical "mystery" by changing the language and the emphasis of research and bringing the needs of these children more clearly into the focus of educators.

The work with autistic children proceeds along a similar course. Both primary theory development and research on the nature of the organic substrate of the condition and programmatic research must move ahead together.

The programmatic work on educational services for learning disabled children resulted in several important outcomes with significant implications for the education of autistic children. Among the outcomes of this stream of educational history which contribute to the development of educational curricula and methods for autistic children are the following: diagnostic and prescriptive education; attention to the stimulus value of curriculum materials and the assumptions a curriculum makes about the adaptive ability of the learner; task analysis; perceptual motor training curricula; the importance of structure in relationships and curriculum; programming for the use of intact sensory channels to circumvent specific sensory deficits; the development of language training curricula, and the development and refinement of psychoeducational and developmental diagnostic instruments and procedures.

The learning disabilities movement, which emerged from the study and education of children with presumed brain injury, has produced a very substantial base of technical, procedural, and curriculum knowledge which is of instrumental value in developing educational services for autistic children.

PROFESSIONAL ISSUES

The passage of P.L. 94-142 raises many professional issues in special education which are not peculiar to autistic children, but which affect them along with other children needing and having a legal right to a free appropriate education. Two of these issues will be discussed briefly in this section: advocacy and the integrity of service delivery.

Advocacy

Advocacy has become an important force in the delivery of services for handicapped children. It is a movement which, in the late sixties and early seventies, had its roots in the civil rights movement of the sixties. It attempted to represent the interests and perspective of the child and to make the service delivery system more accountable in responding to his needs (Paul, Neufeld, and Pelosi 1977).

P.L. 94-142 was, in part, a result of the advocacy efforts of many parent organizations. The Developmental Disabilities Construction and Services Act amendments of 1975 included autism in the definition of developmental disabilities primarily as a result of the advocacy efforts of the National Society for Autistic Children (NSAC).

The basic philosophy of the broader advocacy movement did not, however, obtain support of the parents of autistic children. Advocacy was for all children and not for a particular group. Many parents of autistic children felt they had had experience with programs for "all" children, and the evidence was clear: their children did not receive benefits from these programs.

At this point some advocacy functions have been somewhat institutionalized within governmental structures such as state developmental disabilities advocacy councils. But essential advocacy functions are still necessary in private structures outside the service delivery system. The NSAC serves this primary advocacy function for autistic children. The larger and more complex the service delivery system becomes, the more the need for external monitoring and intervention to maintain service quality and efficiency.

A major component of the advocacy movement is legal advocacy (Turnbull 1978), which has been the tooth of the advocacy movement. Coupled with the political advocacy of parent organizations at the state and national level, and personal advocacy of benefactors at the local level, legal advocacy will continue to be an essential part of the total advocacy effort.

Integrity of Service Delivery

It has become increasingly clear that the nature and philosophical orientation of services and the place where they are delivered is extremely important to the consumers of those services. Humanistic logic and data are very clear on this point. Four major aspects of this general issue of the integrity of service delivery will be discussed here: normalization, deinstitutionalization, mainstreaming, and service integration.

NORMALIZATION

Normalization is a philosophy of service delivery which, according to Wolfensberger (1972), was originated by Bank-Mikkelsen, director of the Danish Mental Retardation Service, in 1959, and later elaborated by Nirje, then director of the Swedish Association for Retarded Children. The basic idea was to help the mentally retarded live as close to normal as possible.

The central thesis is that deviant behavior of many handicapped persons is, in part, a function of the cultural deviance of settings in which they are treated. The culture of institutional settings, for example, is so discontinuous with the normal culture in social expectations, rules, procedures, and artifacts, that the client or patient does not have an opportunity to learn adaptive behavior and values that will work in society outside the institution. Normalization is the antithesis of institutionalization.

For autistic children who frequently spend at least some of their developmental years in residential institutions, the concept of normalizing the setting and optimizing opportunities for normal socialization is very important. In view of the primary communication deficits of autistic children, it is predictable that institutions will defer to the pathology and develop accommodations that are unnatural and would be found only in institutional settings. These must be resisted if the institutionalized child is to improve.

DEINSTITUTIONALIZATION

Recognizing the problems in providing quality care in large institutions, the United States has made a substantial effort to reduce institutional dependency since the early seventies (Paul *et al.* 1977). In a national study involving leaders in the child mental health field, Hobbs (1975) concluded that large institutions are not good vehicles for the delivery of quality services.

There have been three foci to this movement: (1) to prevent institutional placement, (2) to return those placed in institutions to their own community where possible, and (3) to improve the environments of institutions for those for whom no other service is available. A major necessary strategy has been to develop alternative living arrangements and services in communities. This has been only partially successful.

The improvement of institutional environments and services and the development of services in the community that preempt the necessity for institutionalization will continue to be important for autistic children. Interdisciplinary parent and family support systems, respite care, and parent collectives which provide advocacy for individual children are essential to making deinstitutionalization work for these children. Autism cannot be prevented given today's scientific knowledge of its cause(s). Long-term institutionalization, which in many instances compounds the developmental problems of these children and further reduces the likelihood of any adaptive functioning in society, can be substantially reduced. We do know how to do this and why.

MAINSTREAMING

Mainstreaming is to the educational system what deinstitutionalization is to the health, mental health, and social welfare systems. It is an ecological strategy, an intervention that focuses on the system. Mainstreaming is a slogan in education that has been used to describe the movement of children as close as possible to the regular classroom (Paul, Turnbull, and Cruickshank 1977; Pappanikou and Paul 1977). With the rapid development of special education in public schools during the sixties, many mistakes were made. Many children were wrongly placed in special classes and these classes often were misused. System policies and procedures allowed children to be labeled and removed from their normal peer groups and placed in environments where they suffered the stigma of segregation and were not provided a demonstrably better educational experience. The legislative provision that children be provided an appropriate education in the least restrictive environment (mainstreaming) is, in effect, an attempt to remedy errors in educational policies and practices. The fear has been that this would mean all children should be served in the regular classroom. That was not the intent, and it would be folly, from an educational perspective, to try to implement such a principle, especially for autistic children.

The mainstream is wherever a child can succeed educationally. If that is a special class, then the special class is the mainstream for that child.

The mainstream for the autistic child is not the regular classroom. However, mainstreaming is important to the autistic child, because it guarantees accountability in placement decisions including involving the parents. It assures periodic review and opportunity to move as the child's progress indicates, and it reduces the number of children inappropriately placed in settings and using resources that are needed by autistic children. The system must be mainstreamed in order for all children to have optional opportunity for educational benefits (Pappanikou and Paul 1977). Clearly, from this perspective, autistic children will be better served as a result of mainstreaming.

SERVICE INTEGRATION

Autistic children and their parents (as much as any consumer group) have been victimized by the lack of communication and coordination between agencies. The complexity of the problem of autism, the relatively little knowledge, until recently, of effective clinical and educational procedures, and the failure of a single service system to assume primary case management responsibility have created for parents a serious problem in obtaining services.

When services were made available, they were frequently expensive and often ineffective. The already burdened family was frequently further exasperated by the long-term treatments which produced little significant gain. It was, indeed, this collective frustration of parents that caused them to organize and more aggressively pursue courses of political and legal advocacy.

There have been attempts at, for example, developing a "single portal of entry" into the service delivery system or more recently, designating a "lead agency." The very multidisciplinary nature of the problem of autism and the multiagency support required places the autistic child and his family into a strong bureaucratic headwind. Territorial boundaries do separate service systems which compete for funds. Human service agencies do not "naturally" get together, share records, or, in many instances, even talk the same language. The nature of the multidimensional problem of autism and the bureaucratic nature of human service organizations are such that many of the problems in continuity of professional services are predictable in the absence of plans to prevent or remedy those problems.

Many attempts at service integration are under way using systems approaches to planning, budgeting, and operations. A fundamental solution to this problem, however, still seems far away.

Until a broad-based solution is found, several approaches are workable at local and even regional levels. These include community organization and liaison approaches, such as those developed in project Re-Education, interdisciplinary training and service centers such as those in the TEACCH program in North Carolina, and individual advocacy.

While much of the service integration problem is in the delivery system itself, a large part of it is in the failure of professional training programs to prepare professionals with an interdisciplinary perspective and sense of values. Many professionals do not know how to use other professionals or to contribute their expertise to other professionals as a member of an interdisciplinary team. This is a long-term problem of training and resocialization of the professions. Many training programs are beginning to attack this problem. The university-affiliated facilities, for example, are addressing this problem directly on a broad scale.

Recent federal legislation is having a profound impact on handicapped children, their parents, and on professionals. A new and dramatic chapter is being written in the history of human services and in the professional issues involved in delivering educational services to autistic children and their families. New professional alliances, responsibilities, and behaviors are being required. The remainder of this chapter will focus on the nature of the legislation which brings new life, opportunities, and complexities to educational services for these children.

LEGISLATION

Legislative action has and will continue to have major impact on educational services for the handicapped, including the autistic. The 1960s and the 1970s have seen an increase in activity by the U.S. Congress with regard to handicapped persons. Significant pieces of legislation have been voted into law to insure the civil rights of the handicapped, to guarantee a right to a free, appropriate public education, to provide vocational rehabilitation services for even severely handicapped persons, and to provide comprehensive services for developmentally disabled persons. Additional bills have focused on medical screening and treatment needs.

Laws characteristically interact with one another in a manner indicative of the concept that "the whole is greater than the sum of its parts." That is, various laws, when combined, provide more protection or greater service delivery than any of them singly, or than any of them when viewed strictly in an additive sense. The U.S. Congress has enacted legislation which will affect the total environment in which the handicapped individual lives. The focus has shifted from expecting change of the handicapped persons to altering the systems and environment to fit the needs of the handicapped.

Important legislation which will have an impact on the lives of the autistic include P.L. 89-313, which provides money to state institutions; Titles XVIII and XIX of the Social Securities Act Amendments, which provide medical care; P.L. 92-424, which requires enrollment of handicapped children in Head Start programs, and P.L. 93-112, which provides vocational rehabilitation services, providing more services for severely handicapped persons. These mandates by Congress provide the background for two other major legislative acts which were signed into law in 1975. These actions signaled "the end of the quiet revolution" for the legal and human rights of the handicapped (Abeson and Zettel 1977). A brief description of the legislation follows.

Public Law 89-313 was enacted in 1968. One section of 89-313 provides federal monies to institutions for the mentally and physically handicapped, specifically for the education of their residents. These monies follow the residents into the communities if and when they leave the institution for alternative community placements. These federal monies are supplementary to that amount provided by the state for basic educational services. They are administered by the state agency in charge of the institution. Once the resident leaves the institution, the local educational agency (LEA) takes administrative control of the funding. Obviously, the provision is aimed at better educational services for the institutional population. It also represents congressional awareness of such issues as the normalization principle and deinstitutionalization, by reducing the likelihood that the residents will be penalized for leaving the residential facility for a more normalized community placement.

Congress has provided other support for institutionalized populations and for those in need of long-term medical care. Titles XVIII and XIX (Medicare and Medicaid) of the Social Security Act amendments are two such examples. Medicare (Title XVIII) provides health insurance for Americans 65 or older and for many disabled persons under 65. Title XVIII helps to pay for inpatient hospital care and for certain follow-up care after leaving a hospital. It can help pay for doctors' services, outpatient hospital services, and meeting other medical needs for those disabled who are eligible.

Medicaid (Title XIX) is a grant-in-aid program under which the federal government reimburses costs incurred by states in providing medical care for those who cannot afford it. In addition, states may elect to pay for medical care provided to medically needy persons and families, defined as individuals whose income equals or exceeds the state's standards under the appropriate financial assistance, but is insufficient to meet their medical needs. Included in the services which states must provide are inpatient and outpatient hospital services, laboratory and x-ray services, skilled nursing home services, Early and Periodic Screening, Diagnosis, and Treatment (EPSDT) programs, physician services, home health care services, and family planning services.

Title XIX requires states to take an aggressive stand in preventive medical services for children by way of the EPSDT programs. It requires that states seek out those in need of services, with the rationale that early diagnosis may aid in preventing future problems. Title XIX, at the option of the state, may also include nursing home care for children and care in Intermediate Care Facilities (ICF). Many public and private institutions for the mentally retarded and other handicapped persons can qualify as ICFs for inclusion in the benefits of Medicaid, but must meet Medicaid-prescribed ICF/MR standards. Thus, these two titles require certain quality assurances as well as providing financial aid.

In 1972 P.L. 92-424 amended sections of the Economic Opportunity Act (the Head Start legislation) by requiring that 10 percent of the children served be handicapped. Requiring enrollment represented a different approach by Congress. It indicated a growing awareness in Congress to the needs of disabled populations and represented a change in the focus from money to rights. This focus has carried over into other legislation, such as the Vocational Rehabilitation Act of 1973. Section 504 of this act requires that any program receiving federal financial aid must provide services to the handicapped just as it provides them to any other individual. Federal financial aid is defined as anything other than mortgage guarantees.

> . . . no otherwise qualified handicapped individual in the United States . . . shall solely by reason of his handicap be excluded from the participation in, be denied benefits of, or be subjected to discrimination under any program or activity receiving Federal financial assistance. (P.L. 93-112, Sec. 504)

These words represent the most comprehensive statutory provision prohibiting discrimination on the basis of handicap ever passed by Congress. Section 504 is a comprehensive mandate to protect the civil rights of the handicapped. It prohibits discrimination in any program of any kind which receives federal funding. As such, it complements all other legislation which might deal with discrimination against the handicapped in education, employment, or any other area. Because this provision has been so controversial, the final regulations were not signed until March of 1977 by HEW Secretary Joseph Califano.

The laws just described present a picture of the federal law which provides for the rights of the handicapped. Section 504, specifically, protects the rights to services for the handicapped. However, two more recent federal acts have taken a step beyond protection. They have not only protected the right to services and treatment, but have mandated that these services be appropriate for the handicaped persons. Together these two bills signal more comprehensive and more appropriate services for the developmentally disabled and better enforcement of their rights.

P.L. 94-103—Developmentally Disabled Services and Construction Act (DDSA)

In 1975 amendments to the 1970 Developmentally Disabled Services and Construction Act were passed. The new sections of the law are referred to as P.L. 94-103. These amendments join with the 1970 version of the law to form the most recent direction which Congress has chosen to take in procuring comprehensive, coordinated services for the developmentally disabled. The following description is a compilation of the original and amended sections of this legislation, referred to as the DD law. According to the DD law:

> The term "developmental disability" means a disability of a person which is attributable to mental retardation, cerebral palsy, epilepsy, or autism; is attributable to any other condition of a person found to be closely related to mental retardation because such condition results in similar impairment of general intellectual functioning or adaptive behavior to that of mentally retarded persons or requires treatment and services similar to those required for such persons, or is attributable to dyslexia resulting from a disability described in this subparagraph; originates before such person attains age 18; has continued or can be expected to continue indefinitely, and constitutes a substantial handicap to such person's ability to function normally in society. [P.L. 94-103, Section 401 (11)]

The DD legislation has impact on all persons defined as developmentally disabled and on their families and the providers of services to them. Basically, the law mandates three general provisions:

1. A DD council is to be created in every state and territory in the United States, to be composed of one-third consumers (those who are themselves developmentally disabled or their next of kin who represent them). The expressed role of these councils is to serve as consultants to

the state agency for development and periodic review of state plans for the provision of coordinated comprehensive services for the developmentally disabled. The DD Council has full approval power over the State Plan, which includes how it is to be implemented.

2. Mechanisms are to be developed for the protection and advocacy for the developmentally disabled. These requirements include the generation of individualized habilitation plans (IHP) for all persons served, development of protection and advocacy (P and A) systems to protect the rights of the handicapped, enforcement of required service standards for residential facilities, and investigation of standards and quality assurance mechanisms for residential and community facilities.

3. Special studies of the definition of the developmentally disabled are to be initiated.

In addition to these major provisions, the law provides that a percentage of each state's federal allotment of monies for the developmentally disabled shall go toward the elimination of inappropriate institutionalization. The legislation highlights deinstitutionalization. The movement of Congress toward deinstitutionalization, as indicated earlier, was manifested in the passage of P.L. 89-313. In that act the provision of money for education services followed a resident of an institution into a community placement. The DD law directly requires states to use a portion of their funds to seek new means and methods for deinstitutionalization.

In addition, the amendments to the DD law now give the DD councils the power to review federal and state plans for services for the developmentally disabled.

This legislation which includes autism as developmental disability is important to the autistic, their parents, and the professionals who serve them. The DD legislation mandates that services for those defined as developmentally disabled be comprehensive. For the first time, the autistic must be regarded legally when plans are being made for services. The intent of the definition is functional in the sense that services are to be based on shared *needs* of people with long-term handicapping conditions that occur early in life rather than on clinical categories.

DDSA also requires deinstitutionalization for the autistic when possible. The National Society for Autistic Children (NSAC) recognizes the normality of expecting a child to grow and leave the home and the need for services to make this possible.

It is the position of the National Society for Autistic Children that, except in cases of obvious medically indisputable incapacities, all effort should be exerted to encourage public and private agencies and parents to develop as many alternatives as possible for private living and working communities or workshops, giving any possible opportunities for more capable adults to leave the sheltered living aspects of the community to rejoin public life, if possible, while providing at the same time, opportunities to return evenings, weekends, and holidays to the centers for the opportunities for socialization, continuing education, recreation and a chance for a reasonably normal life away from an institution or home, no matter what the degree of impairment. (NSAC, 1971)

Generally, the DD legislation benefits the autistic in three ways. First, it recognizes the autistic as developmentally disabled and in need of services. Second, it insures parental participation (via the DD councils) in reviewing statewide plans for services for the developmentally disabled. Third, it includes the autistic in the search for alternative community placement.

P.L. 94-142—The Education for All Handicapped Children Act of 1975

On November 29, 1975, President Gerald R. Ford signed into law the Education for All Handicapped Children Act of 1975 (P.L. 94-142). This law is the result of lobbying efforts of many individuals and groups (including NSAC) and follows a history of court battles over the right to education beginning with the now historic *Brown v. Board of Education* case. Basically, the law insures a free, appropriate public education for all handicapped children 3–21 years of age. In many sections the law closely reflects the history of litigation over education which preceded it. In 1955 the Supreme Court upheld the ruling in *Brown v. Board of Education*, which struck down the "separate but equal" education policies of the time. This ruling gave *every child* the right to a free public education. Twenty years and many legal battles later, the Congress gave every child, *including the handicapped*, the same rights. Once again, Congress is reaffirming its stand that handicapped persons must enjoy the same freedoms and rights as any other American citizen. However, 94-142 does more than insure the right to education. The bill presents incentive grants to state (SEA) and local education agencies (LEA) to educate preschool handicapped children. It requires that every child be educated appropriately, and places the burden of proof on the state.

The major provisions of the bill are: (1) the right to education for all handicapped children; (2) the right to a free, appropriate education; (3) the right to non-discriminatory testing; and (4) the right to due process. What does all this mean? First, it means that no handicapped child may be excluded from receiving a public education. It is illegal to exclude a child because there are no programs which fit his needs. The onus is taken off the child and placed on the education system. Programs will have to be tailored to suit a child in the public schools or the school system will have to pay for that child to receive a private education at no extra cost to the parents. This concept is termed "zero reject."

Second, the child will not only be educated in the public schools, but this education must also be "appropriate" and in the "least restrictive environment" possible (Pelosi and Hocutt 1977). Appropriate and least restrictive education will be assured for each child by the requirement that each child receive an individualized educational plan (IEP) which sets forth the short- and long-term goals for the child, the services which the child will receive, and the degree to which the child will be able to participate in the regular programs offered by the school. An IEP as defined in the law is:

> A written statement for each handicapped child developed in any meeting by a representative of the local educational agency or an intermediate educational unit who shall be qualified to provide, or supervise the provisions of specifically designed instruction to meet the unique needs of handicapped children, the teacher, the parents or guardians of such child, and whenever appropriate, such child, which statement shall include [A] a statement of the present levels of educational performance of such child, [B] a statement of annual goals including short- and long-term instructional objectives, [C] a statement of the specific educational services to be provided such child and the extent to which such child will be able to participate in regular educational programs, [D] the projected date for initiation and anticipated duration of such services and appropriate objective criteria and evaluation procedures and schedules for determining, on at least an annual basis, whether instructional objectives are being met. [P.L. 94-142, Sec. 4, a, 19]

The IEP is designed to insure that the LEA be accountable to the child and his parents for the quality and appropriateness of the child's education. It also creates a system for periodic checks on the appropriateness of the services being offered and on the success of those services.

The IEP is not a contract, however, so teachers cannot be made accountable if the child does not reach the goals set out in the IEP. The IEP requires that information on the child's present educational functioning level be obtained by instruments and methods that are non-discriminatory. In the case of the autistic, this regulation obviously will cause problems as few, if any, tests have been validated or standardized with autistic populations. However, it is intended to safeguard the child from undeserved negative labels as a result of an inappropriate and insufficient assessment process. This regulation is aimed at preventing categorization on the basis of a single assessment instrument. It will focus assessment on behavioral observations, including input from the parents, on the child's level of functioning. Parents have been found to be accurate in their assessment of the educational functioning of their children (Schopler and Reichler 1972; Copobianco and Knox 1964).

The regulations of this law provide parents with an outlet for dissatisfaction with the educational system. Parents are given rights to due process, including guaranteed access to all records that deal with the identification, evaluation, and educational placement of their child. They are entitled to obtain an independent evaluation of their child by an examiner of their choice. The parents may initiate a due process hearing to present complaints regarding placement or testing. They may be advised by counsel or by an individual with expertise related to the education of the handicapped. Beyond the due process hearing, parents may appeal to the SEA for the review and may take civil action if still not satisfied.

P.L. 94-142 is a major legislative action for the education of handicapped children. For the autistic there are some specific points to be considered. First, the Education for All Handicapped Children Act specifically denies that any child is uneducable. It defines education in a broad sense as a continuous process by which individuals learn to cope with their environment. For the autistic this means that achievement is no longer the private burden of the child and his parents. The burden is now shared by professionals who must seek appropriate methods and services for educating these children.

Second, the new law requires that those who have been unserved are first priority in receiving services now. Second to the unserved in priority are those who are the most severely handicapped. The autistic benefit from these priorities, since many of them have been denied services in the past and are among the most severely handicapped.

Third, the new law requires that parents be involved in the child's education. Parents have been released from the position of guilt into which they had been placed by some professionals and have taken their rightful position as guardian of the child. The resources of parents are being recognized in the law. The responsibility of parents for their child's welfare is underscored in this legislation in the form of parent control over treatment and education plans (IEP) for their child.

Fourth, the law requires that the child receive an education in an environment which is the least restrictive available. This will require school systems to provide a number of alternative programs to fit the needs of the child. It also provides the child with opportunity to experience as normal an educational setting as possible.

Fifth, the law provides a grievance procedure by which parents may indicate their dissatisfaction with the educational services provided to their child. It legitimizes the parents to have an impact on the educational system.

The purpose of this chapter has been to provide a perspective on the development of educational responsibility for autistic children. For those interested persons, further information regarding the laws presented in this chapter may be obtained by contacting any Congressman requesting a compilation of the law.

6

EDUCATIONAL PROGRAMMING

Ronald Wiegerink

and

Maria Paluszny, M.D.

Uɴᴛɪʟ the last decade, most autistic children were institutionalized. These children were generally considered unmanageable and uneducable. However, as a result of research and improved clinical practices, we can now state without equivocation that autistic children can benefit significantly from education. While the prognosis for individual autistic children varies considerably, educational approaches appear to benefit the autistic child more than any other type of intervention.

Unfortunately, the work on understanding the educational needs of autistic children just like other work in autism, has been spotty. The field has not proceeded in a direct course from understanding etiology to developing a treatment plan. Instead, research on etiology and attempts at educational planning developed independently of each other. Until recently advances in neurophysiological studies remained as isolated pieces of information. This knowledge was useful in exploring possible causes of autism but was not being translated into practical therapeutic techniques. Intervention techniques were often developed based on behavior modification methods using little if any understanding of the perceptual problems present in autism. Currently integration of theory and practice is becoming a reality. Many treatment programs and intervention techniques use data on neurophysiological deficits to establish treatment methods that circumvent this handicap. We shall cite here some of the evidence of specific neurological dysfunctions that pertain to special educational techniques. We shall discuss some general educational factors influencing approaches and present specific approaches and types of educational programs.

ETIOLOGICAL FACTORS INFLUENCING EDUCATION

Recent studies and detailed analysis of apparent neurological problems

115

in autistic children are important in current educational programming (Gallagher and Wiegerink 1976). Such studies have demonstrated that autistic children have difficulties in a variety of cognitive areas. Often they cannot use symbols (Pibram 1970), and this may be one reason for their lack of language development. In addition, these children possibly do not receive consistent integrated stimulation from the outside world. The work of Ornitz and Ritvo (1968) suggests that autistic children may at times be bombarded by excessive stimulation which they cannot screen out, while at other times the same children may be unable to receive sensory input and thus are completely unresponsive to external stimulation. Other studies have indicated that autistic children have difficulties in memory and recall (Bryson 1970, 1972) and cannot extract rules to code or make generalizations (Hermelin 1976).

A number of researchers have focused on the autistic child's sensory modalities and how he uses them differently from other children. For example, problems in auditory processing of information have been noted. Others found that autistic children use some sensory modalities such as vision far less than other modalities such as tactile manipulation of objects (Hermelin and O'Conner 1970).

These and other similar observations are all exceedingly important when we remember that the major function of special education is to teach the child through techniques which circumvent learning difficulties while accentuating or building on the intact areas. In autistic children, because of the numerous deficits finding areas to build on is often a problem. Techniques that work with one autistic child may not always work with others. For this reason, general educational strategies are often used in addition to more specific methods.

GENERAL EDUCATIONAL APPROACHES

The learning behavior of any child is often influenced by circumstances other than his innate ability or any existing handicap. Factors such as student-teacher relationship, the pupil's maturity, and environmental circumstances can and do influence the classroom situation. Problems in any of these areas are often compensated for by the average child, but in a class for handicapped children, great care must be taken to reduce any additional interferences to learning. In addressing these issues, various investigators have suggested how to improve the learning environment for the autistic child.

THE TEACHER

In assessing the factors influencing a teacher's ability to teach autistic children in a behavior modification setting, researchers (Rincover and Koegel 1975; Koegel and Rincover 1976; and Koegel *et al.*1977) found the following skills to be particularly important:

1. The teacher must know how to present instructions correctly. These instructions should be clear, consistent, and brief.

2. The teacher must know how to present reinforcers effectively. A reinforcer should be given immediately so that the child will soon associate the correct response with the reward.

3. The teacher should know how to "shape" a new behavior. By shaping a behavior it is meant that the teacher rewards initially gross responses which are an approximation of the desired response. Gradually, the teacher records narrower, more economic responses which are closer to the ideal response. Finally, by this process, the ideal response is reached. In order to do this, of course, the teacher must be able to break down the child's responses into graduated steps. An example of shaping could be the teacher's asking the child to bring him or her a book. Initially, the child may be rewarded for making a motion toward an object; later the child may be rewarded for bringing an object, and finally the reward would come when the child brought the specific object asked for—the book.

4. The teacher should know how to prompt or guide the child to respond correctly, then to fade out that prompt when the child is responding on his own. For example, in getting a child to bring a book, the teacher may initially hand the book to the child. Later the child can be prompted by taking him by the hand and leading him in the desired direction. Finally, when the child responds correctly, the physical prompts are not used but verbal control in the form of saying "bring me the book," is instituted.

5. Finally, there should be a time interval between learning one task and beginning another. During this interval, responding is not required and the child has a chance to internalize the learning experience without being distracted and confused by a new instruction.

In addition to the above skills, teachers of autistic children should have certain important personality characteristics. It must be remembered that in a program for autistic children the teacher functions to a great extent as a therapist and in order to be effective in this role, the teacher must be able to inspire confidence. This is especially important with autistic children where the parents often look to the teacher for guidance regarding the management of the child's behavior in the home.

In addition, patience in dealing with the child and an ability to communicate with the child's parents are personality factors which can determine the success or failure of a teacher as much as any of the skills outlined.

MOTIVATION

Autistic children are typically withdrawn and preoccupied with their own stereotypic activities. Often just interfering with these isolated activities is a problem; substituting other activities presents a major hurdle. In many programs attempts have been made to increase the autistic child's motivation for learning by using a variety of powerful reinforcers such as food (Risley and Wolf 1967) and pain reduction (Lovass, Schaefer, and Simmons 1965).

However, problems sometimes arise in using such artificial reinforcers. Since these reinforcers are specific to the teaching or training situation there is no natural transition to the child's home environment. As a result children seem to discriminate between these two environments and tend not to carry over the behaviors or skills they learned at school to the home setting. In addition, food in particular has a self-limiting usage. After a period of time, children become satiated and another piece of fruit or candy is no longer a significant reward.

To overcome such problems, some investigators have turned to other types of reinforcers. In this respect, certain sensory stimulation appears to be a promising substitute for the use of food. For example Rincover, Newsome, Lovaas, and Koegel (1977) have used music and strobe lights as reinforcers. The children were motivated to learn language skills when strobe was presented as a reinforcer. When they appeared no longer interested in the strobe light (satiation had occurred), it was found that the child's interest could be again reinforced by changing the frequency of the strobe.

In some higher functioning autistic children, physical contact such as stroking and hugging can be used as a reinforcer. Often this is done together with verbal praising, and eventually the physical component can be faded out with the verbal portion becoming the primary reinforcer.

Various investigators have used other methods to increase motivation. In general, however, reinforcers which can be provided easily, occur naturally in the child's environment, and can be used readily in the school, home, and other settings have a greater chance of success over time.

DECREASING INTERFERING BEHAVIORS

If a child is preoccupied with another activity, obviously he cannot attend to learning. Even normal children may show periods of unresponsiveness because of anxious "fidgetiness" or episodes of day dreaming. The autistic child, however, is usually preoccupied with his own world and often involved with his own form of self-stimulatory behavior. To increase learning, this competing activity must be decreased. The extent to which self-stimulatory behavior can interfere with other activities was demonstrated by researchers (Newsom 1974) who found that after autistic children were taught to play with toys they only played when self-stimulatory behavior was suppressed. This occurred even without a reinforcer. However, if the children were free to choose their activity, they invariably chose the self-stimulating behavior over the play behavior.

A major task for any teacher working with an autistic child is to determine how to stop the stereotypic self-stimulation. Different approaches have been tried in this respect, varying from negative reinforcement to ignoring the behavior and thus it is hoped, allowing it to fade. One of the more promising methods in this respect has to do with determining why the self-stimulating occurs in the first place. One of the theories in this area is that autistic children receive certain sensory stimulation from their environment in this manner. This stimulation is more predictable than other types of stimulation since the child has control over the initiation and cessation of the activity. With this in mind, a type of sensory extinction can be set up. For example, one child who constantly twirled or spun objects on hard surfaces stopped these activities when the table was carpeted. Cushioning the surface prevented his usual auditory and possibly other sensory feedback which had previously been the reinforcer for this activity (Rincover 1978). Later, this child was taught to use more appropriate play behavior by selecting activities and toys which gave him the same sensory input.

Another way of achieving the same objective of preventing self-stimulatory behavior is to develop a competing behavior which the child will find more rewarding. Care must be taken, however, that this new behavior will lend itself to modification so that it can be used as the first step to a learning process and not an end in itself.

STRUCTURING AND SETTING SESSIONS

The way teaching sessions are organized and conducted can be very important in focusing the autistic child's attention and helping him learn. To aid the child in anticipating the sessions the establishment of a particular routine of both time and place is useful. It has been suggested that careful repetition of a routine builds security and trust in the teacher and the program itself (Bachrach 1978). Structuring the session is also connected with more favorable results. This is especially true in working with the more regressed autistic child (Schopler *et al.* 1971), but even in less regressed autistic children, clear expectations coupled with a didactic approach in a structured setting seem more effective than a nondirective permissive approach (Bartak and Rutter 1973; Rutter and Bartak 1973).

The setting in which the teaching session takes place is important. Usually a room with few distractions is used, and some researchers have even suggested focusing on specific modalities by decreasing the input from others. For example, Fassler and Bryant (1970) found the use of sound protectors similar to ear muffs useful with some children. The child's attention is focused on the teacher by having the teacher sit close to the child (but not so close as to be threatening). It has even been suggested that sitting side by side may be less threatening than the teacher facing the child (Taylor 1976). In beginning sessions, the child and teacher work often 1:1; however, once the autistic child has mastered some skills, groups of children may be instructed together (Rincover and Koegel 1975). Often such group instruction is basically parallel learning with little child-to-child interaction, yet in such situations the opportunity to build or enhance social interaction is nonetheless always present.

In many instances group instruction forms the basis of existing educational programs for autistic children. Some of these will be considered later in this chapter; first, however, we shall discuss some specific educational strategies used with autistic children.

SPECIFIC EDUCATIONAL APPROACHES

Currently, behavior modification techniques either alone or in conjunction with other approaches are frequently used in the education of autistic children. Since this approach was discussed in Chapter 4, in relation to the management of behavior problems, a detailed description will not be presented here. Rather, this section will deal with some specific skill development used with autistic children as a way of circumventing or minimizing their handicaps. The two major strategies to promote skill development focus on development of various sensory modalities and on the development of communication skills.

Development of Sensory Modalities

A number of teachers and investigators have addressed the issue of the autistic child's lack of exploration of his environment, unusual preferences in sensory modalities, and apparent lack of awareness of his own body and its limits. Keeping these problems in mind, strategies have been developed to enhance the autistic child's use of his senses. In the early stages of his development (as described by Wood 1975) the child is taught to respond to his environment with pleasure. In this approach the child is given tactile, kinesthetic, visual, auditory, gustatory, and olfactory stimulation so that he can learn to respond with various sensory modalities. Initially, just a response is desired. Later, both the response and the stimuli become more complex; for example, initially the child may just attend to a single sensory stimulus but later activities are geared to develop both motor and total body response to complex environmental and verbal stimuli. The teacher's role in this exploration of self and environment is an "arouser," someone who provides satisfaction and nurturance. In later stages the teacher will have different roles—as someone who aids in organizing routines, as a model for group participation. The emphasis in later stages shifts to different skills. This general program will be discussed in more detail later; at this time, however, it is important to note that the primary focus of this approach is on the sensory modalities.

Other workers with autistic children have taken the same path of working with sensory modalities as a prerequisite to more complex skill development. Such approaches are described by Miller and Miller (1973) and Taylor (1976).

Guided by the as yet unproven theory that developmentally disabled children first learn to direct body action, later learn to use distal senses, and finally develop language and thought toward objects, Miller and Miller (1973) devised a program to enhance body awareness. In this training program, boards were elevated and connected with obstacles, tunnels, and bridges to guide and maneuver children to solve problems of activity. The child has to open doors, lower drawbridges, slide down, push-pull, pick up, and sometimes jump. Thus, a variety of motor activities were provided in addition to an "edge" experience. The edge experience was achieved by suspending boards three to six feet above the ground so that the child was forced to become aware of himself in relation to his environment. When the child demonstrated he had learned intention activity (he was aware of being elevated and could do the various motor activities to get through the obstacle course), then signs were used which the child had to demonstrate in order to proceed along the course.

For example, for a drawbridge to open the child had to demonstrate "open" by opening his hands. Eventually when the child learned to use signs above ground they were then taught to use the same signs in everyday situations on the ground. Finally, spoken words were substituted for the signs. In the final analysis though these were individual differences, all children learned to respond and express themselves by signs. Likewise, all children responded to some spoken words; however, only a few learned to express themselves verbally. Taylor (1976) suggests promoting visual skills is an important step in teaching skills underlaying language development. She suggests the teacher should not pressure the child but with quiet approval present developmental tasks in game-like fashion. The simplest of these games strengthen visual-motor coordination and let the child learn that there are rules governing the relationships between objects. For example, the child may be given a box with a hole which is big enough to pass small beads but not big ones. If the beads are of different colors, the child can learn not only that one size will not go through but also learn to associate this size with a color. Gradually, more complex games are introduced to teach the child skills like left to right sequencing, matching objects and rules underlaying associations. Eventually the child learns associations of ideas such as cup and saucer and grouping of objects using concepts. Even learning cooperation can be presented and these lead to labels which are the precursor of language.

From the above examples it can be seen that stressing sensory modalities may be an important early step in teaching autistic children more complex skills. A major complex skill which is emphasized in many programs is the development of communication.

Verbal and Nonverbal Communication

Problems in language development are characteristic of autistic children. Only about 50 percent develop speech, and even those show the typical problems of echolalia (repeating what is said to them), pronominal reversal, and the use of stereotyped phrases. Even more advanced autistic children use repetitive questioning, tend not to use speech for spontaneous communication, and often miss subtleties since their use of language is concrete. The problem is not just in expressive language but in comprehension. Language in its broadest definition is affected—not just understanding and production of speech, but the total area of nonverbal communication is involved. Because of the seriousness of this difficulty some investigators have suggested this lack of communication may be a major factor in the atypical behavior of autistic children (Casey 1978).

A number of techniques have been developed by workers to teach the autistic child communication. These include the use of sign language, the use of devices to teach reading and writing, and systems to increase and improve verbal communication.

Sign language has been used by some workers in teaching communication to mute autistic children. As autistic children often have difficulties in making auditory-visual associations yet have relatively few difficulties in the motor area, this method appears particularly appropriate. Creedon (1973) was the first to use sign language with autistic children. Later other investigators used sign language with positive results. Though there are differences in technique, the method generally used is a type of behavior modification. If possible the stimulus chosen is one that is self-reinforcing. For example, in teaching a child to sign for "cookie" a cookie was used as a reinforcement. With this method in one study a nonverbal autistic child learned a number of words by sign language learning at the rate of approximately one new word in every two sessions (Salvin *et al.* 1977). Both in the above study and a subsequent one (Casey 1978) an important aspect was the close cooperation of the teacher and parents to maintain the manual sign program both at home and at school.

Teaching sign language to autistic children has several advantages, among the most important being the develoment of a communication system between the child and parents so that the child can be instructed in what he *should* do rather than just being punished for what he *should not* do. In addition, if and when the autistic child learns verbal communication, sign language can be faded out as regular speech develops.

Occasionally mechanical devices have been used to aid the autistic child in learning communication skills. For example, Wiegerink and Mort (1970) used an electric typewriter to teach the autistic child to communicate by writing. The child could first explore the typewriter to familiarize himself with the equipment and also to gain his interest. Later the teacher called out specific letters and turned the electric switch only if the child picked that letter. Much later when the child learned a set of letters the teacher presented alphabet cards and called out the letters. Still later names of objects were presented. Finally, pictures of objects were presented and the child would type out the appropriate name.

In teaching speech most teachers start with precursor skills such as reinforcing eye contact, imitating behavior such as gestures, promoting sound production, and finally moving to repetitive speech and spontaneous speech. In most teaching programs the principles of reinforcement, shaping, and fading are used (Hewitt 1965; Risley and Wolf 1967). One such program, that of Ivar Lovaas at UCLA, will be described later in greater detail.

In summary the teaching of communication skills whether by sign language, actual speech, or by some other method, is often a critical approach to the special education of the autistic child. Frequently, whatever other approaches are used some form of communication training is included.

SPECIAL PROGRAMS

Slowly more and better educational services are becoming available to the autistic child within the community. Ideally such programs will include detailed assessments of the child's intellectual abilities, sensory and cognitive deficits, language ability, emotional maturity, and behavioral problems. Such programs should take into account the child's skills and attributes as well as deficits, and an individualized curriculum can be developed around these strengths and weaknesses. However, generally these community programs are just beginning, and in many instances revisions will be necessary before they are fully functioning.

Often the community or local programs are modeled after some programs for autistic children which have been in operation for several years. To present an overview of different programs the following will be described: The Development Therapy of Rutland Center, RIP of Nashville, TEACCH Program of North Carolina, Behavior Research Institute (BRI) Program, the Judevine Center Program, and the Language Program as described by Ivar Lovaas.

DEVELOPMENTAL THERAPY AT RUTLAND CENTER (GEORGIA)

A basic assumption of this program is that the autistic child needs more normal models. Thus, in addition to an intensive highly specialized program at the center, the autistic child is concurrently placed in other programs serving children. Once accepted, the child is enrolled with a group of six other children who are at the same developmental level. Classes are conducted five days a week, two hours a day. In addition, the child has a daily school experience and also a structured therapeutic session with his parents. After the parent observes the child working with a therapist the parent is taught how to handle this activity with the child. At home the parents practice this activity, then at biweekly sessions the parents demonstrate to the staff how they conduct the activity.

The curriculm of the development therapy program consists of sequences of developmental tasks aimed at improving the child's functioning in four major areas: (1) behavior, (2) communication, (3) socialization, and (4) pre-academics. Each one of these areas is divided into five stages of specific objectives arranged in a hierarchical fashion representing successively higher functioning in that area. Each of the five stages has a different emphasis, and different techniques are used.

Stage I—Responding to the Environment. In this stage the teacher is the person who arouses and satisfies. Through physical contact, stimulating activities, the use of body language, and other techniques, the child is taught to respond and trust the environment.

Stage II—Responding to the Environment with Success. Here the teacher redirects behaviors so that the child learns individual skills and experiences success. The emphasis is on routines and consistency in behavior. Ordering and classifying concepts are introduced in the pre-academic area.

Stage III—Learning Skills for Group Participation. The focus is on groups and how rules apply to groups. The consequences of behavior are outlined, and an attempt is made to approximate real life as much as possible. Verbal skills for expression are emphasized.

Stage IV—Investing in Group Processes. The children take more active roles, with the teacher acting as a group leader. Role playing is explored, and outings and field trips are planned and carried out in this stage.

Stage V—Applying Skills to New Situations. Here the child is taught to generalize from experience and to solve new problems. For example, in the socialization area the child will be taught to initiate peer relationships.

It should be remembered that this model of therapy is highly individual, since a child may be functioning in one stage in one area and at a different stage in another area. Thus, despite the children's being in a group, careful monitoring of each child's progress is maintained. Details of this program and the techniques used have been published in two books (Wood 1975; Bachrach *et al.* 1978).

THE REGIONAL INTERVENTION PROGRAM (RIP)

A statewide program centered in Nashville, Tennessee, for autistic children and their families (Weigerink and Parrish 1977) emphasizes training parents to work with their preschool children. Many of the children are autistic, but other handicapped youngsters are enrolled. Parents are instructed in behavior modification procedures for instructing their child.

The setting is used to aid in increasing positive social interaction between parent and child.

There are four different classrooms in this program, each utilizing parents under the supervision of professional staff. The classroom settings include an intake classroom, a toddler classroom, a language classroom, and a community classroom. Each classroom is designed to instruct in specific areas of development. The intake classroom focuses on appropriate classroom behavior associated with following a typical classroom schedule and routine. The toddler classroom focuses on sensorimotor skills and elemental language behaviors (one-word responses). The language classroom provides for a varied group and individualized language program which supplements each child's individual clinical tutoring. The community classroom emphasizes social play behaviors and prepares the child for public school and developmental day care settings in the community.

RIP has been a site for numerous studies of strategies for increasing social interaction among handicapped children (Strain, Timm, and Wiegerink 1974; Strain and Wiegerink 1975, 1976). Each study explores classroom and group procedures for making education of autistic children more effective and efficient.

TEACCH PROGRAM OF NORTH CAROLINA

The Treatment and Education of Autistic and Related Communications of Handicapped Children Program is another program which uses parents as co-teachers and co-therapists. The parents participate both in classroom activities and also carry out specific training activities in the home (Reichler and Schopler 1976).

The program is statewide and was established by the North Carolina Legislature in 1972. It consists of five clinical diagnostic and treatment centers located in the five major population areas of the state and eleven special education classrooms distributed across these regions. Each classroom, located in community schools, provides an educational program for five to eight children. These modified self-contained classrooms provide tailored developmental programs for each child. Children are also provided with the opportunity to participate in certain regular classrooms when it is appropriate to their needs and abilities. The class also serves as a resource room for other children in the school with communication handicaps. These children not only receive instructional help but provide social interaction for the autistic children. Treatment is sometimes continued in a clinical setting but this varies according to each child's needs. Each classroom is staffed by a teacher and an assistant who are inservice trained by the TEACCH staff. Likewise, the parents are trained by the TEACCH staff so that approaches are similar and continuity is maintained in all aspects of the child's life.

JUDEVINE CENTER PROGRAM

This program centered in St. Louis provides local services, services for out-of-city and out-of-state children, and a training component for professionals. The program has been in operation since the early 1970s. A variety of severely disturbed children are admitted, including autistic, retarded, schizophrenic, and children with atypical development or severe behavior problems. In the evaluation both the children and parents are assessed. The primary focus for this assessment and later treatment sessions is based on "social exchange" principles (see Chapter 4). Parent-child and parent-teacher interactions are carefully recorded, analyzed, and modified where needed. The child's behavior is modified to behavior which will elicit the response he wants, whereas the adult's behavior is modified to encourage the production of desired behavior in the child and to discourage or extinguish inappropriate responses.

The areas of training focus on (1) physical aspects such as ambulation and manipulation, (2) social aspects such as rapport, communication, and responsibility, and (3) intellectual aspects such as information, ideation, and creativity. Each child's curriculum is based on deficits or needs in each of these areas. Training areas are broken down into smaller components and specific procedures, which are arranged sequentially. Progress is monitored by definite criteria. In addition to the children in the program, parents, teachers, and other personnel have expectations mapped out for them.

Each child progresses through five treatment levels, each of which includes more children and takes longer periods of time. For example, level 1, which stresses compliance with instructions, may focus on maintaining eye contact. Such sessions may last only twenty minutes and be conducted in a 1:1 ratio. More complex levels such as level 4 may focus on competitive play or completion of tasks without supervision. A class for level 4 training may involve only one teacher to five students, and each session may last three to five hours.

The parent training program typically lasts three weeks (90 hours of training). Out-of-state parents are typically enrolled in this part of the program. The program consists of observation, didactic material, assistance in applying the skill, and, finally, the parent applying the skill independently (O'Dell and Blackwell *et al.* 1977).

THE LANGUAGE DEVELOPMENT PROGRAM

A number of authors have focused on different aspects of programs for autistic children in and around Los Angeles (Graham and Flaharty 1976; Los Angeles County Autism Project, Needels and Jamison 1976). This brief description focuses on the language program as described by Lovass (1977).

The program's basic technique is operant conditioning. The basic theoretical stance is that language is acquired through the child's ability to recognize certain stimuli as giving rise to verbal production. Such stimuli may be internal or external, but in either case, once a verbal utterance is produced a response occurs (another behavior, verbal utterance, etc., is produced either by the child himself or others). This view of language relates it to discrimination learning and to Skinner's (1957) view of language, though not all authorities in the areas of language or autism agree with these concepts. In treating autistic children in this program an assumption is made that the "autistic child's failure to acquire language is based on his deficient motivational structure" (Lovass 1977, p. 33). Thus interfering behaviors are first eliminated; then, by the systematic use of positive reinforcement and aversive stimuli, language is built.

The program consists of eight subprograms arranged from simple to complex with some overlap in various areas.

Program 1—Building Verbal Responses. Imitation of verbal utterances is taught. No meaning is elicited and the productions are generally echolalic.
Program 2—Labeling. A basic vocabulary is taught so that the child can label everyday objects and events.
Program 3—Relationships. Spatial relationships (prepositions), time concepts, pronouns, size, shape, and other abstractions which describe relationships are the focus of this program.
Program 4—Conversation. The child learns to ask and answer questions and to make comments about things to the teacher.
Program 5—Information. The aim here is to help the child to gain information about his environment by asking questions and by giving answers.
Program 6—Grammatical Skills. As the program becomes more complex, the child obviously needs to use phrases and sentences. In this program he is drilled on rules governing sentence structure.

Program 7—Recall. This is an enriching experience where the child can also learn from and share his past with others. He is taught to recall and describe past events.

Program 8—Spontaneity. Here the focus is not on a specific response but on letting the child describe in a manner that allows him some choice. For example the child may be asked what he had for breakfast. The expected answer would include not just an itemized listing but comments on how the foods looked and tasted and if the child enjoyed it.

The above summaries of programs are just a glimpse of how they function. There are many other programs not described here, yet the ones mentioned reflect the variety and similarities of the field.

In describing these programs the aim is not to endorse or recommend any or all of these. The comments about each program are not based on objective evaluations but rather on the information available from each center.

At this point a word should be inserted on how parents can choose an appropriate program for their autistic child. Certainly the reputation of a center is important, but it is also advisable to visit the center and gain a firsthand impression of the staff and setting. In assessing a center three factors are the most important from a parent's perspective. These are:

1. Concern for the individual child. The staff should be aware and concerned about the child as a person and an individual and not as just a diagnostic entity. If negative reinforcement is used, this should be carefully monitored and should involve the parent's consent and approval.

2. Curriculum or planned strategies. The center should have specific objectives for each child and clearly defined steps of how these goals are to be reached.

3. Evaluation of approach. Within the prescribed objectives adjustments must be made if the child is not progressing at the expected rate. Thus careful monitoring and modification must be built into the programs.

Most of the effective programs blend individual and group instruction and a behavior modification or prescriptive teaching format. They use a developmental framework of starting with elementary behaviors of attending to the more complex behaviors of language and social interaction, combine the teaching of autistic children with other handicapped and non-handicapped children, and involve parents as partners and teachers.

These programs are largely directed to what Rutter (1970) suggested as the three goals of education for the autistic child: (1) preventing the development of secondary handicaps; (2) finding approaches to education that circumvent the primary handicaps; and (3) finding techniques to aid the development of functions involved in the primary handicaps.

It can safely be said that in the last decade we have made giant steps toward these goals. The gap between research on etiology and the development of training programs is being decreased. The knowledge of the autistic child's sensory, coding, integrative, language and other neurological problems is slowly being translated into therapeutic training programs. Effective educational programming for autistic children is no longer a dream; it is a reality. The next and most important goal is making it a reality for all autistic children and their families.

7

PARENT INVOLVEMENT

Marie Bristol
and
Ronald Wiegerink

T HE PARENT'S role in the syndrome of autism has been the subject of much discussion since Kanner defined the syndrome in 1943. Although Kanner first spoke of autism as an "inborn defect of affective contact" this theory was soon overshadowed in his work as well as in the work of others by the idea of the "refrigerator parents" whose rejection of the child during a critical period was in some way a cause of autism.

Early research studies of parents of autistic children relied on indirect measures of parental personality and attitudes and compared parents of autistic children with parents of normal children. As a result of such studies, parents of autistic children were purported to be "cold," "mechanical," "insensitive to the needs of the child," "overprotective," or "cynical, obsessive, and passive." Parents who asked questions, gave directions, and structured situations were said to be "intrusive." Those who did not were said to be "perplexed."

The role the parent played in the treatment of the autistic child depended on the extent to which he or she was seen as the "cause" of the child's autism. Therapists such as Bettelheim, who saw parents as the primary cause of the child's "withdrawal," advocated what Schopler calls "parentectomy," or the complete removal of the child from his parents and treatment in a residential setting with parent substitutes. Other therapists who believed in the parental pathology thesis advocated less radical, but no less pejorative treatments. As a condition of receiving treatment for their child, parents were often urged or even required to undergo long periods of psychotherapy or psychoanalysis focusing on parental characteristics or practices that might have caused the child's autism. Parents who refused were considered to be uninterested in their child's welfare. Refusal itself was seen as an affirmation of parental pathology.

As more research was done on autism and controlled studies on families of autistic children replaced "clinical impressions," the findings demonstrated that parents of autistic children are essentially no different

131

from other parents. Furthermore, careful studies on autistic children themselves produced more and more evidence of a primary neurophysiological dysfunction. Currently the preponderance of informed professional opinion subscribes the "cause" or "causes" of autism to an unknown organic impairment rather than pathology in the parent-child relationship.

Once the parents were no longer seen as culprits, they became increasingly important as part of the therapeutic team in working with the autistic child. In fact, in a follow-up study of autistic children treated at UCLA, Lovaas and his coworkers (1973) found that children whose parents had been trained to carry out interventions at home continued to make progress after leaving the formal program. Children without such trained adults in their environment not only failed to make continuous progress, but even regressed to pretreatment levels. The concept of parents as co-therapists or teachers of their own children is now firmly established as a hallmark of most of the successful programs described in this book.

OVERVIEW OF THE PARENTAL ROLE

The changing role of parents in the treatment of autism is largely the result of three major trends: (1) mounting evidence of a biological basis for autism; (2) lack of empirical support for psychogenic theories and psychoanalytic treatment; and the (3) development of behavioral interventions.

Biological Basis for Autism

As evidence for a biological basis for autism began to mount (Ritvo 1976; McNeil and Wiegerink 1971) and the case for a purely psychogenic causation became less tenable, various authors began to parcel out the guilt and suggested that parents might be the cause of only the "nonorganic" form of autism, or that parental pathology might cause autism only in biologically vulnerable infants. However, early studies that reportedly distinguished organic from nonorganic cases have not been replicated even by authors such as Goldfarb who originally reported them.

The idea of biologically vulnerable infant and defective caretaking is in keeping with the notion of a continuum of caretaking causality proposed by Sameroff and Chandler (1975). Unfortunately, however, no case has ever been reported of a "biologically vulnerable" autistic infant who received proper care and grew to be normal. At the present time there is no evidence that any kind of parenting could have prevented the development of autism in an organically impaired child. In fact, studies that have analyzed factors influencing a better prognosis suggest the amount of schooling the child receives is critical, whereas parental factors do not seem to influence outcome (see Chapter 1).

Lack of Empirical Support for Psychogenic/Psychoanalytic Parent Theories

A variety of strategies has been used to test the link between parental pathology and the child's autism. Researchers have investigated the relationship to the etiology of autism of severe early trauma, parental attitudes toward childrearing, parental personality deviance or thought disorders, and deviant parent-child interaction. With few exceptions, studies which used an adequate diagnosis of autism and included a handicapped rather than a normal control group found no evidence that parents of autistic children were abnormal or engaged in parenting practices which should have "caused" their child's autism.

Rutter, Greenfeld, and Lockyer (1967) found that only 9 percent of autistic children came from single parent families as compared with 22 percent of children with other forms of psychiatric disorders. Similarly, Bender and Grugett (1956) found that both "broken homes" and "poor emotional climate" were less frequent in the backgrounds of young schizophrenics and autistics than in the histories of children with other psychiatric disorders. No significant differences were found on any of the measures of early stress when histories of autistic, dysphasic, and normal children were compared by Cox, Rutter, Newman, and Bartak (1975). Parents of autistic children did not report more maternal depression during the child's first two years, nor were parental deaths, divorces, separations from the child, or financial, housing, or health stresses more common for parents of autistic children than for parents of the comparison groups.

An alternate strategy related to the early trauma theory has been to follow children known to have experienced early deprivation or stress. Although institutionalization, hospital admission, and separation experiences have been shown to be related to substantial increases in psychiatric disorders, cases of autism among these populations are virtually nonexistent (Rutter 1968). The evidence clearly indicates that early trauma is not a sufficient or necessary explanation for the autistic syndrome.

In a retrospective study of childrearing attitudes, DeMyer and her coworkers (1972) found no evidence of rejecting parenting attitudes or practices among parents of autistic children when parent responses were compared with responses of non-psychotic subnormal children. Other authors have found similar results.

Creak and Ini (1960) and Schopler (1973) have found parents of autistic children to display the normal range of personality characteristics and a normal range of reactions to the extraordinary demands of being the parents of an autistic child.

Schopler (1978) reviewed the results of approximately 100 studies and concluded that the publications linking autism and schizophrenia to parental pathology are significantly time-bound, the majority of them having been published before 1965. He suggests that the research question in these studies was cast in such a way, at least partly, to confirm the prevailing psychoanalytic theory which tended to explain both normal and deviant personality development in terms of early family experience.

Much of this would be merely of historical interest except that many, if not the majority of professionals interacting with parents of autistic children received their own training under the same prevailing *zeitgeist*. In spite of the fact that there is no evidence linking autism to deviant parental behaviors or attitudes, nor is there any evidence that psychotherapy or psychoanalysis either for the child or the parents has been effective in significantly improving the child's status, many professionals continue to operate on the basis of psychodynamic assumptions regarding the etiology of autism.

The Development of Behavioral Interventions

The dramatic successes achieved with autistic children through laboratory applications of the operant procedures described in preceding chapters were cause for a great deal of optimism. It was soon apparent, however, that the hard-won gains of the autistic child were fragile, indeed. New skills often did not generalize outside of the original treatment or learning setting and were quickly lost once treatment was discontinued.

It was clear that if gains were to be maintained outside the treatment setting, it would be necessary to have a trained person in the child's natural environment to extend his learning to new situations. The cost of having professionals assume such a role was clearly prohibitive; furthermore, the shortage of such professionals made this plan untenable. A person was needed who had strong reinforcing properties for the child, control over the child's significant reinforcers, and was available for extended contact with the child. The logical person to fill such a role was, of course, the parent. Parent training programs described by Wiegerink and Parrish (1977); Schopler and Reichler (1976), Kozloff (1973), and Bristol

(1977) no longer considered parents as patients but rather as partners. Although most of these programs involved training parents in center-based settings, other authors have described programs in which the training takes place directly in the child's home (Hensley *et al.* 1978).

PARENTS AS TEACHERS

The best parent training programs utilize the same principles of good teaching described in the preceding chapter. In the program for behavior disordered preschool children at the Southeast Mental Health and Retardation Center described by Bristol (1977), parents are involved in all stages of the child's treatment program. In the evaluation process the parents provide a developmental history by giving their assessment of the child's functioning in five developmental areas. Then, in a structured session, the parents interact with the child so that the parent's interaction style and the child's responses can be observed. Following initial assessment training sessions are done jointly with the parent or parents, the child, and the therapist. At first, the parent merely observes the therapist as he or she works with the child. Gradually, the parent assumes more of the direct responsibility for the child's session and the therapist is faded to an observation room where the parent can be coached with a wireless transmitter or "Bug-in-the-Ear" device. When the parent has learned the principles of giving clear instructions, shaping or prompting a response, reinforcing correct responses, and extinguishing incorrect or inappropriate responses, the parent is then given programs to carry out in the home. Where distance to the center is prohibitive, the original training is done in the child's home and a therapist makes regularly scheduled home visits to assist the parent in implementing programs in the home setting.

At the mental health center, in addition to training in behavior modification, there are various parent education and discussion groups aimed at helping the parents in a number of areas. The topics of these sessions range from specific suggestions, such as what activities can be used to promote language development, to global issues, such as forming advocacy groups of parents of autistic children.

Parents as Learners

Designing education programs for parent groups of autistic children involves more than merely planning the content or curriculum. Special problems of distance and diversity are encountered in building such parent support groups. Often only a few parents of autistic children may be found in one area; such groups may be diverse in socioeconomic status—urban versus rural background—and even in their expectations of the groups' function. In addition, it is clear that it is a relatively easy task to change parents' vocabularies, but a much more difficult task to get parents actually to experiment with new behaviors with their children. Traditional lecture methods of parent education tend to attract or at least retain only relatively articulate, middle-class parents who are comfortable in large groups, yet the goal is to aid all parents of autistic children. To overcome some of these obstacles a rather novel approach was developed by Gingold and McDonald in the Southeast Mental Health Center program. Parent education clubs were formed in parent homes, drawing on the parents' natural network of friends or relatives. A parent initiator is trained in group dynamic skills and is provided with learning packets containing a short introduction to a topic, together with a list of activities for each parent to carry out at home with her child relevant to the behavioral or developmental topic covered at the last meeting. For attending meetings, for getting their spouses to attend meetings, for carrying out suggested activities with their child or for generating new activities, parents receive PACT (Parents and Children Together), dollars (play money) exchangeable for educational toys for their children chosen from a catalog of toys arranged according to developmental level.

The center staff act as consultants to the parents, providing materials, films, or speakers during the eight-week sequence or beyond for those "alumni" groups that choose to continue. Different sets of materials are available for normal and handicapped groups. The groups provide not only a learning experience, but the opportunity for mutual sharing and support among parents as well as a chance for some parents to develop leadership skills. A recent group for parents of handicapped youngsters was led by a parent initiator who was deaf but verbal. She proudly reported that her group had 100 percent attendance for all eight sessions. The Head Start groups that have been involved in this rather novel approach note that attendance at these meetings is double that at their usual parent education meetings. The cost of such a program averages approximately $35 per parent. We hope that it is a long-term investment forming the nucleus of a parent-to-parent support network that continues after the parent is no longer in contact with the Mental Health Center.

This project also provides a Lekotek or toy lending library. The library is housed in the public library and staffed by the junior league. Toy library staff and participating parents receive training in the choice and use of toys in encouraging child development.

In programs such as the one described above, or in TEACCH and RIP which have been described in previous chapters, parents are clearly partners in the therapeutic or educational process. In this context, parents are important not only in implementing programs for their child, but also in choosing treatment objectives and designing the interventions. This is, of course, a gradual process, one involving much demonstration, feedback, and support.

ENLISTING PARENTAL SUPPORT IN PARENT TRAINING PROGRAMS

For those contemplating implementation of programs designed to train parents to be teachers or therapists for their own children, there are a number of pitfalls to be avoided.

Parental Priorities

One major cause of failure in some programs is neglect of parent input in establishing priorities for the child's program. Before a teacher or therapist concludes that a parent is not being "cooperative" in carrying out a suggested program or home intervention, the therapist must ask if the program meets the family's needs as well as the clinic or school's. A parent concerned about a child's setting fires during the night can hardly be blamed for not being concerned about teaching the child shape discrimination. To insure continued parent participation, interventions must focus on problems which are important to the family. Research has demonstrated that parents who are committed to program goals are more likely to follow through in carrying out activities, will become more skilled as teachers, and will be more likely to have children who show measurable progress (Rosenberg 1977).

Often, priorities parents set are different than those set by teachers or therapists. Parents often choose target behaviors such as toileting as most important while teachers may see such problems as less important, and may have little or no experience in such areas. Thus it is helpful to have a multidisciplinary team work with the family so that a large pool of skills is readily available. Initially, it is also critical to choose simpler behaviors that will respond quickly to treatment, leaving the more complex behaviors till later when the therapist or teacher has established his or her credibility with the parent. Likewise after some positive results, the parents will have more confidence in their ability to succeed. For this reason, it is often helpful when teaching parents behavior modification techniques to have them practice the techniques or principles first on a normal child. The normal child will typically respond more quickly, giving the parent immediate reinforcement and more confidence in the technique. Early training should also include both acceleration (learning) and deceleration (extinction or reduction of behaviors) in order to teach the parent the learning model.

Maintaining Parent Commitment

Another major problem in enlisting parents as therapists or teachers of their autistic child is the lack of reinforcers available to them. Theoretically, the reinforcer for the parent's involvement in the child's program is the subsequent change in the child's behavior. This might be satisfactory when working on bizarre or disruptive behavior where the results are fairly immediate and often dramatic. It is much more of a problem when the parent is asked to carry out complex speech or language programs where progress may be painfully slow. In such cases, it is important for professionals to deliberately plan ways to support the parent. Occasionally methods such as supportive phone calls from the worker or the encouragement of another parent who has already "been there" may be useful. In all parent-as-teacher-programs a two-way communication system is essential. In addition to the professionals ongoing support and new input the parent must have a system to alert the professional when the program needs to be adjusted or the parent needs extra support.

The Less Active Parent

A corollary of respecting parental priorities is the realization that the success of parent programs depends as much on the support of the less active parent as on the one who is actively involved. A home program designed by the first author to eliminate the throwing of objects by a three-year-old boy can be used to illustrate this point. At first, for no apparent reason, the program appeared to be a dismal failure. Review of data provided as a parent graph suggested that the program was somehow being sabotaged by the father's presence. A meeting with both parents revealed that the father considered his son's throwing to be the "one normal boy thing" that the child did. The program was revised to take the father's priorities into account with a specific time and place set for "free throwing." More importantly, both parents established a priority listing of target behaviors for intervention. This enabled the therapist to obtain both parents' perceptions of the child as he was presently functioning and as they would like him to be. Such a procedure enables the therapist or teacher to be aware of discrepancies in both parents' perceptions or expectations.

One milestone in successful adjustment to having a handicapped child is learning to have realistic expectations for the child. The importance of this step cannot be overestimated, but helping parents to reach this point takes the utmost professional concern and care. The professional must help the parents give up unrealistic aspirations for the child, but not discourage the parents so that they feel it is not worthwhile working with the child. Learning to have realistic expectations for a handicapped child is a difficult and gradual process. Cansler, Martin, and Valand (1975) discuss the three stages of adjustment parents move through in accepting their child's handicap. Cansler suggests that parents first deny that the child is handicapped or is as severely handicapped as they have been told. Gradually, intellectually, the parent is able to face the truth, but reacts with anger, guilt, depression, and grief. Finally, the parent is able realistically to accept the child and his handicap both intellectually and emotionally. Both mother and father are not necessarily at the same stage in their movement through this process. Often the expressed parental expectations and the degree to which each parent is willing to be directly involved in the child's treatment reflect which stage of acceptance the parent has achieved.

In dealing with parental expectations, the teacher or therapist must not overlook the parents' real need for specific information as well as emotional support. Whenever possible, interpretive and other parent conferences aimed at giving specific diagnostic, prognostic, and treatment information should include both parents so their expectations can be as uniform as possible.

One of the most critical requirements for working successfully with parents in their roles as teachers or co-therapists is the realization that this is only one of the roles or demands being made on the parent. The parents have other aspects of their lives which must be kept in perspective. The professional working with the parents must help them to maintain a balance between their role as parent-therapists and their role as parents to their autistic child. Likewise, they must maintain a balance in their relationship to their handicapped child and other relationships and demands of other facets of their lives.

PARENT SUPPORT SYSTEMS

Educational programs have increasingly called upon parents to serve as teachers of their own children. However, an excess of such involvement may be detrimental to the parents' functioning in their primary role as parent. Teachers—especially teachers who have previously worked with more mildly impaired children (as most teachers have)—have typically focused on a rather narrow range of educational goals, essentially those involving academic or pre-academic skills. Parents, previously often the only educational resource for their autistic child, have assisted professionals in teaching these tasks. As schools assume more and more of the burden that is rightly theirs, parent training will be able to focus more on involvement of parents in activities more directly related to parenting and family life. Unfortunately few teachers have been adequately prepared to teach the range of self-help and other home skills needed by the autistic child. Fewer still have been trained to teach parents the interpersonal or affective skills necessary for integrating a severely autistic child into a family.

Thus, in addition to teachers and parents the input of other professionals and non-professionals is helpful in maintaining optimum conditions for the autistic child and his family. Frequently, such a support system can be provided by social workers, parents of other autistic children, and the family support network.

Parent-Professional Interaction

Parents who have not fully accepted the child's handicap are often particularly difficult for inexperienced professionals to deal with. Although they may not have admitted to themselves the extent of their grief, they may vent their anger and hostility on the professionals with whom they come into contact. On the other hand, especially with parents of autistic children, previous experiences with professionals may have been part of an endless merry-go-round of referrals, expenses, and no services. One autistic child with whom the first author had contact had received no fewer than twenty-four different diagnoses. That represented twenty-four visits to various centers, twenty-three of which found the child to be an "interesting case," but "inappropriate" for their program. Professionals who work with parents of autistic children must be prepared to work, not only with their own impact on the parents, but with the parents' accumulated frustrations from their interactions with other professionals. Genuine need for information and demand for appropriate services should be recognized as such. Too often the parents' search is dismissed by professionals as the parents' need to deny the child's handicap or as an effort to shop for a diagnosis the parents would be willing to accept.

Adapting to the Reality of Having a Handicapped Child

A major contribution that both professionals can make in their encounters with parents is helping parents to work with the shock, anger, and grief of finding themselves the parents of an autistic child. Olshansky (1962) speaks of the "chronic sorrow" experienced by families of handicapped children, even after the adjustment process described above has been completed. The sorrow and the stress may not be most acute when the parents first learn of the child's diagnosis, but the sadness is rekindled at other stages of the child's life. For example, when the child's peers go off to "regular" school, or when the adolescent child's aggression overwhelms them, or when they are faced with the certainty that their child will never be able to be competitively employed, and alternative services are not available. When changes occur or such milestones are reached, each family must deal with the anger, grief, and pain before a new family equilibrium can be found. If not, blame and denial will be a wedge between the parents and frustrate efforts at involving the parents in treatment.

Tavormina and his coworkers (1977) have described four major parent styles of adapting to the reality of having a handicapped child. In the first case, the father "emotionally divorces" himself from the child, leaving the care of the child entirely up to the mother and involving himself fully in outside activities such as his job and organizations unrelated to the child. A second style of adaptation is when the parents join together in rejecting the child. The child in this type of family is most apt to be institutionalized, regardless of the severity of his handicap. In the third style, the parents make the child the center of their universe, subordinating all of their own desires and pleasures to the service of the handicapped child. The child is usually quick to sense such an arrangement and to take advantage of it by making the parents feel guilty for wanting a life of their own. The final style is one in which the parents join in mutual support of the child and each other, but maintain a sense of their own identities and a semblance of a normal life. Although the last style seems by far the most adaptive, Tavormina is quick to point out that there is no single best style for all families, or at least, it is unrealistic to expect that all parents will use only this most adaptive style. In fact, it is likely that mixtures of these adaptive styles exist in any one family at different times.

Acceptance of a child and his handicap may often be best facilitated not by professionals, but by other parents who have children with similar problems. Every effort should be made to put parents in contact with other parents of autistic children both through informal parent networks and formal organizations such as the National Society for Autistic Children.* This society maintains a clearinghouse of information on services, provides relevant publications, and sponsors conferences or meetings on the topic of autism.

Family Support Network

Grandparents and other extended family members are very important to the autistic child and his parents. Relatives need to understand the child's condition as well as the parameters of therapy. In most extreme cases the grandparents or other relatives may "blame" the parents for the child's handicap. Such stress on the parents may be eliminated by giving the relatives factual information and even enlisting their help in the therapeutic process. If this fails, however, the professional may need to help the parents to be assertive enough to set limits on the relatives' intrusion.

Occasionally, the grandparents may intefere with therapy by calling mother's faithful adherence to an extinction program as "heartless." In such cases the therapist may enlist the aid of significant relatives in carrying out the therapeutic program. This type of network therapy will not only provide the autistic child with a uniform environment, but also the explanation of the system will aid in dispelling any misinformation or unrealistic expectations the grandparents may have. Involving extended family in the network therapy allows the parents to have more time for other activities and relationships—more time for each other, for other children, etc. Moreover, often grandparents and other relatives find that being active participants in the therapeutic process helps them feel less helpless and possibly helps to relieve any guilt they may experience.

Respite Care

Parents of all handicapped children occasionally need time away from such a child to get adequate rest, revitalize their strengths, and to give some undivided attention to each other and other children. This is perhaps of even greater importance with parents of autistic children where the parents have dual roles of parent and parent/therapist. Respite care is a very important part of the parent's support system. In some communities respite care is provided through short-term hospitalization or another type of in-patient facility. However, if this can be done on an out-patient basis, in the child's own home, the adverse reactions of sepa-

---

*The current address for the National Society for Autistic Children is 306 31st St., Huntington, West Virginia 25702. The phone number is (304) 697-2638.

ration will be minimized. In the Mental Health Center described earlier, a program was established by the professional staff to train babysitters to care for children with special needs. Such a program has many obvious advantages, both for the families, the autistic child, and the community, as high-quality respite care can be effective in preventing institutionalization.

Need for Other Systems

Currently, there is a great need for adequate programs for autistic adults. Though some autistic adults are served through existing educational services or vocational rehabilitation services, many are not so lucky. Special programs need to be explored for such adults to take the burden off the parent in being the only caretaker. One type of vocational program for autistic adults is described in Chapter 8. However there are undoubtedly different types of programs and approaches which can and should be developed.

Medical Services

In addition to special schooling there is also a need to provide careful medical services for the autistic child. Generally most pediatricians are not well acquainted with the problems of autism. Most have had some exposure to the syndrome during medical training but may have no practical experience in the area. Some pediatricians may accept a screaming temper tantrum in their office from a two year old but become irritated when the same behavior occurs in a ten-year-old autistic child. Likewise, some pediatricians can communicate beautifully with nonverbal toddlers yet be very uncomfortable with a nonverbal older autistic child. Thus, the parent should select a good understanding pediatrician. This physician need not be an expert in autism but needs to be someone who can tolerate difficult behavior in a resistive child. Here again other parents of autistic children may be very helpful in locating such a physician. Often it is useful to check if a physician is known for treating children with other handicaps such as retardation. It is likely that such a physician will be more accepting of children who show unusual behaviors.

Dental services are often difficult to find for handicapped children. Many dentists refuse outright to see such youngsters. With this in mind some training centers have made special effort to train their dental students to work with handicapped populations. For example, The University of Michigan Dental School sends all of its senior dental students to ISMRRD for practical experience in working with retarded, autistic, cerebral palsied, and other handicapped children.

In most communities the local dental association or a nearby dental school can usually provide parents and professionals with names of dentists who will treat autistic children.

From the above discussion it can be seen that parents of autistic children can utilize a variety of professionals as well as other parents of autistic children and their own extended family for a support system. However, it is important to keep in mind that the autistic child is only one person in the family and the parents must remember their roles as just "regular" parents.

PARENTS AS PARENTS

Even in an average family the role of parent overlaps with many other roles: teacher, cook, general caretaker, chauffeur, etc., etc. In the family of an autistic child it is quite possible to let the role of teacher and caretaker overshadow all others. Yet, for the health and stability of the family the parents must recognize other family members and themselves as individuals. Even in relating to their autistic child how much should they be a teacher and how much just a regular parent? Often in relation to showing affection the parents have concerns and questions. We shall discuss the specific issue of affective contact briefly here, but other areas of handling the day-to-day-problems of the autistic child would necessitate a much lengthier discussion. This area is exceedingly well covered by Lorna Wing in the book *Autistic Children—A Guide for Parents*.

Affective Contact

One of the most frequently expressed fears of parents whose child has been recently diagnosed as autistic is that the child might withdraw further if the parents attempt to be affectionate with him. This myth, which has fairly widespread currency among professionals as well as parents, is reinforced when the child screams or becomes rigid when he is touched or cuddled. Parents need to know that it is not only all right, but important for the child to learn to have contact with his parents. The child who becomes rigid or screams when cuddled may delight in being tickled or tossed in the air. Parents can also introduce brief, gentle touching during activities that are pleasurable for the child such as while he is eating or listening to his favorite music. The child can be taught to tolerate and eventually to respond to affection from family members. Parents can be taught to teach their child desired behaviors. The value of any activity is relative. Parents can learn to make participation in a more desirable activity contingent on prior completion of a behavior or activity that is less reinforcing to the child.

Although it may be initially repugnant to parents to "force" their child to show affection, it is often necessary to teach parents how to mold a child's arms in an embrace or to teach him to kiss his parents or to shake hands. Initially, it is usually best to teach the child to do this in response to the overture of one or two people, since it may be difficult for the child to discriminate appropriate from inappropriate situations for initiating affection, and unsolicited affection directed toward strangers may be upsetting to others.

Parents often need help from professionals in understanding and overcoming what appears to be the child's rejection of them. It is difficult for parents to love or want to interact with a child who does not reach out to them, who may not call them by name, or who may not give any evidence that he recognizes them in a group of strangers. Professionals can help parents recognize that the child is not withdrawing from them, but rather has not developed the cognitive or attentional skills necessary to form a bond with another person. It is important for professionals to recognize the impact such a child's behavior can have on a *parent's self-esteem* and confidence. This is especially critical in working with parents who have no children other than the autistic child. They may have no source of positive feedback regarding their adequacy as parents. Thus, support by way of explaining the behavior as well as positive suggestions on how to initiate activity from professionals and other parents can be very helpful.

The Family Unit—Siblings

An almost universal concern among parents is the effect of an autistic child on normal siblings. There is little data available directly relating to the effect of autistic children on their siblings, but data on the effect of other handicapping conditions suggest that children are very resilient, and even though some have problems related to having a handicapped sibling many can even grow from the experience (Grossman 1972). Parents, however, must be careful to arrange their lives in such a way as to provide adequate attention to the siblings and not to expect the sibling to assume responsibility for their handicapped brother or sister beyond their level of maturity. There is some evidence that sisters of the handicapped child may be more affected since they are more often relied upon for assistance in caretaking.

Siblings often have unexpressed fears that they too will become handicapped or that when they marry they will have handicapped children. Professionals can help families deal with expressed and unexpressed fears. A model for a sibling workshop, including an agenda, a sample letter to parents, and an evaluation instrument, is presented by Cansler, Martin, and Valand (1975). This week-long workshop was conducted by the staff of a developmental center for moderately and severely retarded children.

The effect of the autistic child on his siblings may be directly related to the adequacy of support services available to the parents. The mother whose child is enrolled full time in a school program and who has access to good short-term babysitting and respite care is more apt to be able to have sufficient time for her other children, whereas the mother who attempts to fulfill all the roles herself with no outside support may find she is just too drained to respond to the needs of other family members.

Parents as Persons

Finally, the professional must learn to deal with the "parent as person," and recognize that the parent has needs that extend beyond that of being a parent. Parents should be encouraged to try to find time to be with one another without the children or to be alone and free to develop some of their own resources. Tavormina and Walker (1976) demonstrated that parents of handicapped children who sent their children away to a two-week overnight camp experience significant psychosocial improvements across a variety of measures. Tavormina and his associates (1975) have also shown that mothers of handicapped children who work at an outside job show significantly fewer psychosocial problems than mothers who remain at home all day.

Thus, it appears outside interests and time away from the handicapped child can have beneficial effects. Possibly those parents who are very involved with their autistic child and resist branching out in other directions can be encouraged to take an active role in the National Society for Autistic Children or a similar parent group. Such groups provide diversion, practical suggestions, additional information, and possibly most important serve as a pressure group to obtain adequate programming for autistic children. Parents can utilize the organization to realize and express their own administrative and other talents, while still being very involved with their autistic child.

In the beginning of the chapter we reviewed research that addressed the question of how parental behavior affected autistic children. More recent studies (Holroyd *et al.* 1975; Holroyd and McArthur 1976) have begun to ask not only what impact these parents have had on their autistic children, but what impact having an autistic child has had on the parents, the family, and its interaction with those outside the family. We do not yet know how this stress is affected by the severity of the child's handicap, the age of the child, or the socioeconomic background of the parents. We do not know as yet all the adaptive strategies and the formal and informal support systems that make the difference between parents who can cope and parents who are overwhelmed with the problems of caring for their autistic child. We can, however, be certain that there is no single strategy, no single pattern that will fit all families equally well.

As professionals, many of us have been trained to be child advocates. If we work with families we must be parent advocates as well. When we involve parents in programming for their children we must ask ourselves if our demands are compatible with parental needs to maintain their self-esteem as persons, to preserve the integrity of their families, and to enhance their contact with the larger community.

Anyone who has worked with parents of autistic children cannot fail to be impressed with their ability to survive and even to succeed in the face of what often seem to be insurmountable obstacles. We should approach such families humbly, and in our zeal to teach them, we must not fail to learn from them as well.

8

FUTURE PLANNING

Since Kanner first reported those eleven cases of autistic children numerous books and articles on autism have been written. After thirty-five years many aspects of this disturbance remain unknown, so many more books will undoubtedly follow. Even Kanner did not expect such a turn of events: "The publication of the case findings of 11 patients was prompted merely by a wish to communicate to my colleagues a number of experiences for which I could find no reference in the literature. It did not and could not occur to me at the time that we were on the threshold of creating unexpectedly and unintentionally a great deal of excitement in the field of child psychiatry" (Kanner 1973, p. 138). But excitement was created. Discussions of this syndrome have been marked by bitter controversies over etiology and therapy. Simultaneously research and clinical work have been instrumental in bringing many diverse professional groups to a common path. Perhaps even more important after an initial rift, the wish to help autistic children is finally becoming a bridge between professionals and parents. Seemingly nowhere in the study of childhood disturbances have the battles been as intense or the unification of diverse groups so extensive.

However, a book on autism seems incomplete without two additional presentations. First, since parents are essential in the total field of autism, we must examine their suggestions. Secondly, autistic children grow up, and program recommendations for autistic adults should be mentioned. In order to provide input from parents a questionnaire was sent to a number of parents of autistic children. A discussion of the responses will serve as input from the parents. Secondly, a comprehensive vocational rehabilitation program at ISMRRD will be presented as a possible model for providing services for autistic children when they reach adulthood.

SUGGESTIONS FROM PARENTS

The suggestions the parents gave in the questionnaire can be divided into "Do's" and "Don't's" for professionals dealing with autistic children and parents of autistic children. Interestingly many of the questionnaires had similar responses and almost none had conflicting recommendations.

Do's for Other Parents

In thinking about their own feelings, especially about accepting the diagnosis of autism, many parents felt it was of some help to share their feelings with other persons. In this regard other family members were mentioned, especially the marriage partner. Most often, however, parents felt the aid provided by other parents of autistic children was invaluable. Joining organizations such as the National Society for Autistic Children was highly recommended. Some parents felt their church group or just praying and a renewed interest in religion was helpful. Ultimately, however, the parents felt each one of them had to come to grips with his or her own feelings. Comments such as "take one day at a time," "don't expect too much too soon," or "maintain a positive attitude" were frequently expressed.

In accepting the autistic child as part of the family parents uniformly recommended keeping the autistic child at home, if at all possible. They suggested being open and honest with other children or extended family in informing them that the child was "autistic" and "slow in learning" or "handicapped with special needs." Some felt quite strongly about including the autistic child in family projects, outings, and vacations. Others, however, cautioned about the need of being away from the autistic child. Some especially suggested this allowed the parents to be more available to other children. This particular area showed most disagreement. However, since the questionnaire revealed no information on the severity of autism the disagreement possibly was purely on that basis. In other words parents who had less severely disturbed autistic children could take them on vacations and felt this should be the pattern. Other parents who had more severely disturbed autistic children needed to be away from the autistic child with other family members. The parents who recommended vacations from autistic children usually recommended a formal respite care program rather than informal arrangements with friends or relatives.

In dealing with the autistic child himself only a few parents suggested specific techniques. Some recommended sign language, the Judevine approach, frequent praise and time out for bad behaviors. One parent suggested having the child clean up after himself as an effective method of toilet training. Occasionally medication was mentioned as a helpful adjunct. Over and over again parents stressed the importance of consistency, routine, and firmness coupled with a loving and caring approach. Many parents mentioned that once self-care skills were established to some degree and some methods of communication were learned the autistic child was much easier to handle. The parents of older (and possibly higher functioning) autistic children felt reasoning and explaining was an effective tool in working with these children.

Don't's for Parents

Generally there were only a few don't's. In fact the major don't pertained to the parents' maintaining patience and keeping their cool. The most frequent suggestion was "don't lose your temper." Others recommended expressing feelings in other ways—"laugh" or "cry" but "don't lose control of the situation" was often the parents' advice. On the opposite side parents cautioned about giving up or being complacent. "Don't accept an unsuitable program" was often stated. One parent was even more open and expressive, stating: "Autism is a political problem. To really get good programming for your child you must learn the game. You must know who has power and how to use the law to get what you need. Professionals can't do it, only parents."

Several parents mentioned unusual techniques as not helping or even making the situation worse. Sensory stimulation such as "walking on oatmeal," vestibular stimulation consisting of "spinning," some medications, and negative reinforcement such as spankings were mentioned.

Do's for Professionals

The suggestions for professionals were somewhat different in that generally there were more suggestions in the "don't" category. The major positive suggestion concerned being honest with the parents. "If you don't know what is wrong, say so" paraphrases the general sentiment. Frequently there was also a hint that many professionals did not know enough about autism and could use more direct experience and reading in the area. The confusion created by conflicting opinions was also mentioned. One parent expressed this quite vividly: "Every one of them knows exactly what you should do with your child, but if you put more than 2 of them together in the same room you are going to get 15 different opinions."

Don't's for Professionals

Being unnecessarily opinionated was probably the most frequent comment. This was somewhat of a surprise, since we might expect the professionals' scrutinizing of the parents as possible etiological agents as being the major complaint. Such a comment was actually quite rare and mostly appeared as a criticism of uncovering psychotherapy which failed to produce results—that is, the criticism was aimed at a technique rather than professionals in general.

As already mentioned specific treatment techniques were occasionally discussed but none stood out as frequent recommendations or not recommended methods. The one exception to this was discussion of aversive consequences. As a group only a few of the parents mentioned this technique. However, the ones that did mention negative reinforcement expressed very strong feelings. The parents cited specific long-lasting regressions in their children due to inappropriate or excessive use of negative reinforcement. A few mentioned the baffling problem of just how aversive should the consequences be? and under what circumstances should one use such methods? These parents were opposed to such techniques except in rather extreme circumstances. Obviously, as mentioned numerous times in this book, such problems would not arise (or at least arise very infrequently) if better communication existed between parents and professionals.

From the above discussion of suggestions from parents of autistic children it can be seen that in essence many of these suggestions point out the necessity of parental involvement in their child's program and accepting the child without being overly optimistic or pessimistic about his condition.

The professional's major need is to be better informed and generally to communicate more effectively with parents. This is true in all disturbances of childhood but perhaps especially so in autism for several reasons. First, historically, because of the earlier suspicion that parents were instrumental in etiology, there has been a rift between professionals and parents, and professionals need to work hard to repair this rift. Secondly, progress in recent years in this field has been rapid, and professionals who rarely see autistic children may not be up to date in this area. On the other hand, parents of autistic children as a group are remarkably well informed. Thirdly, as has been pointed out previously, the most effective program for an autistic child is one in which professionals and parents work closely together.

THE AUTISTIC ADULT

A Vocational Program

The program described here is currently in operation at ISMRRD. It is not a program only for autistic adults; any group of handicapped adults who cannot be served through the usual vocational rehabilitation programs qualifies. All the participants are retarded (with an IQ range of 40–74); some have additional handicaps (several are schizophrenic, one is deaf and two were diagnosed as autistic when they were children). The program described here could be used as a prototype for other programs set up throughout the country to serve those autistic adults who cannot benefit from traditional vocational training.

The program was initially set up to demonstrate that many adults previously considered untrainable by regular vocational rehabilitation centers are, in fact, trainable if additional instruction and support is provided. We felt the programs these individuals were getting through work activity centers were insufficient. Work activity center programs focus exclusively on recreation, which seems to us infantilizing for the mildly and moderately handicapped, since such programs are not geared to prepare the individual for either competitive or sheltered employment. We felt if these adults capable of higher functioning could be moved from activity centers to sheltered work situations, or even eventually to the open work market, then the activity centers would be available for the individuals they should really serve—the severely and profoundly impaired.

In ISMRRD's vocational program, thirty young (age 18–35) men and women are enrolled. All were judged to be untrainable by usual vocational centers. Some came from activity centers, some from group homes, while others were at home not receiving any community services. The initial contact was usually made in their own settings. For several of the clients much of the initial evaluation had to be made in their own homes because they were reluctant to participate in any program away from home. Some of these people were eventually willing to come to ISMRRD for the program, but others would not leave home and our team had to be satisfied just with giving suggestions and recommendations and relying on the families to implement these. This occurred most often with lower functioning clients where both client and parents were reluctant to have the client venture outside of the home. We have continued to follow these people, and there are indications some will eventually be willing to participate in the vocational program at ISMRRD.

The program is implemented by a multidisciplinary team headed by a project director who holds a Ph.D. in educational counseling. Other regular staff consist of educators, a speech therapist, physical therapist, social workers, psychologists, additional vocational counselors and support staff. Not assigned to the team, but available as consultants, are a psychiatrist, general physician, and dentist.

The first part of the program consisted of a multidisciplinary evaluation. During the evaluation general self-care, social skills, and medical status are assessed in addition to pre-vocational skills. A program is mapped out, taking into account individual needs of the clients in each of the above areas. The program itself consisted of sessions of a few hours each day. These were increased so that finally clients spent six hours per day four days a week at ISMRRD.

Whenever several clients showed a need in one or more areas a group was organized to meet those needs. Otherwise, the needs were handled on an individual basis. For example a common need was better understanding of their illness for those clients who had epilepsy. First the clients talked about their mutual concerns, experiences, and understandings of the illness, and then a group meeting was set up with the general physician and psychiatrist to discuss additional concerns. It must be mentioned that in order to do this the individual group members previously spent many sessions in learning a number of skills—taking turns, listening for the response, asking additional questions if more information was needed, and, finally, trying to avoid duplicate questions. It is easy to see where this type of experience can be generalized to other social and work situations.

In the initial work with the clients much emphasis was placed on self-care skills and everyday social skills. Groups were held on grooming and hygiene. The bathrooms in the vocational area are equipped with bath and shower facilties, but we never needed to teach our clients the basics of washing. We did, however, teach one of the group to shave. He was fearful of the noise of an electric shaver and no one had ever attempted to teach him to shave with a safety razor. Initially, of course, he had to examine the razor, learn how to stroke himself without the blade in the razor, learn to lather his face. However, after many such steps he did learn to shave himself.

Other group members needed special help in other areas. For example, one of the clients could not cross a street by himself. Through the process of breaking this activity down into small segments, with reinforcement at every step, he finally learned to cross with traffic lights and also streets without traffic lights. Many such examples could be cited, all of them illustrating the many needs our clients have in areas other than vocational.

Quite early in the program we found that praise, especially praise from other group members, was a very effective reinforcer. Thus, we encouraged the development of a group spirit whenever possible. Useful in this regard was the development and supervision of activities which the group members suggested themselves. For example, in the spring, summer, and fall many expressed an interest in jogging. Having first checked out their medical status, we then organized a group who went jogging for up to half an hour each day. Most important in this regard were structured group sessions which specifically focused on interpersonal interaction. In these sessions the group eventually was able to talk about feelings and even progressed to the area of sexuality.

After this initial stage, however, we encountered some serious problems. Although many of our clients made some gains in adaptive behaviors, most clients showed frequent absenteeism and much time spent in chit-chat and other non-task activities. Immature behaviors inadvertently were perpetuated, and the clients showed excess clapping and yelling when they accomplished something, while crying and pouting resulted if a minimal frustration occurred.

On the basis of these largely negative results, it was felt that the expectations and basic tactics of the program had to be changed. The emphasis was then shifted to pre-vocational and vocational training in a highly structured environment.

It should be mentioned that pre-vocational aspects were present to some degree in the first part of the program. For example, the clients had learned to follow instructions, had learned the equivalency of money, etc. However, in those early stages these skills were not emphasized but were taught more in a context aimed at developing social skills. Now, with the shift of emphasis, vocational skills became of paramount importance. In addition to emphasis on discrimination skills, sequencing, and following instructions, a simulated high-demand work environment was created. Money was used as a reinforcer, since most of our clients responded well to the use of money and money is the normal reinforcer in the usual workaday world.

Depending on the client's ability, gross and fine motor work was used—car-washing, lawn mowing, and bench assembly. Bench assembly is the primary focus in winter, and the operation has gradually become more and more complex. In teaching new items we use the systematic application of usual training procedures—modeling procedures (demonstrating what is to be done), priming (using client's hands to go through the motions), chaining (step-wise having clients complete more of required maneuvers), verbal cues (calling attention to errors and suggesting correct ways), and finally faded trainer involvement. All assemblies are task analyzed to allow for step-wise completion. The clients are currently working on the assembly of bicycle brakes and bullwinkle assembly (a type of valve used in portable toilets; its assembly is complicated in that eighteen pieces are required, and in addition, a pneumatic screwdriver must be used). Thus, in effect, our clients are now at the stage of learning skills not usually taught to the handicapped population.

In the three years the program has been in operation, seven clients have been placed in sheltered workshops. Three have been placed in sheltered enclaves (specially supervised sections in general industry), and one was placed in competitive industry. Five dropped out of the program. Most of these had severe emotional problems, and though their ability in actual learning was as good as, or even better than, the group who completed the program, we were unable to discover reinforcers which kept their work rate and quality at a uniform level; their production level could not be maintained on a consistent basis.

Currently, the program focuses on training new clients, but the clients who are already placed are followed on a weekly basis. With this group we found the major concern is neither work situation nor social adjustment, but rather increasing concerns over the appropriate use of money. These clients have no experience in handling money, and as they begin to earn a reasonable wage, many are already looking into the future and anticipating more independence. Since managing money is one aspect of such independence, we not only found problems related to money itself, but often ambivalence and concerns in the general area of independence became expressed as money-related issues. Thus, we anticipate continued counseling with our success group as well as with our ongoing clients.

The type of program described, which focuses on skill development, consistent structure, reinforcing environment, and support in individual areas of weakness, is suited to the autistic adult as well as the severely learning disabled and the retarded individual. We believe similar programs could be constructed through a variety of agencies to serve those individuals who are now seen as not responding to a rehabilitation process.

However, in developing such new programs it should be emphasized that the aim must be at achieving behaviors which will allow the client to function in an environment close to that present in the community. We found that a highly structured environment, which does not allow the client to leave his work or allow the client to exhibit infantile behavior, is best. In fact, the absence of such an environment and orientation may account for the low levels of success reported by sheltered workshops and other work oriented facilities in successfully training and subsequently obtaining productive behavior from lower functioning and autistic clients.

Living Arrangements

In discussing future planning, many parents of autistic children are concerned with what will happen if, as an adult, their child is not ready for independent living. Currently, there are more and more group homes which accept individuals with varying physical, intellectual, and emotional handicaps. Certainly, any such placement has to be pre-screened for adequacy of care and program, but generally these facilities are becoming more geared to providing the least restrictive environment. As local communities become more accepting of handicapped individuals, facilities are allowing more flexibility. Those individuals who can go out by themselves to various community activities (shows, sports activities, and even bars) are often free to do this with minimal or no supervision. Basically, in the more progressive group homes a plan is mapped out for each individual so that he or she can be gradually integrated into the community. For example, in work situations the person may initially be transported by the facility to a sheltered workshop. Later, less supervision is provided, step-by-step, so that eventually the same person may use public transportation to go to a regular job. The same principle of increasing independence can be applied to social relationships. Characteristically, however, even those autistic adults who do well in other areas experience much difficulty in interpersonal relationships. Thus, this area may lag behind the development of other skills, even in an "ideal" group home setting.

For any autistic adult, just as for any autistic child, respite care should be available. In many group homes, possibly several places should be reserved for those autistic adults who live with their own families. Such short-term placements would be most useful if the term of placement can be very flexible. For some, only an occasional evening away from home will be necessary; for others, a few weeks will be needed so that the remaining family can take a vacation. If families had more facilities with respite care available, undoubtably more autistic adults could be maintained in the home.

CONCLUSIONS

The study of autism has progressed greatly since the syndrome was first described in the 1940s. The epidemiology has been described, and though no specific etiology or treatment has been found, the correct approach has been identified. After some false starts, it now appears clear that this organic handicap can be minimized through special education techniques. Such techniques are being continually refined as the search for the specific cause or causes continues.

Possibly more significant than any of the above areas of progress has been the important progress made in integrating the various approaches, research, and work done in autism. At last, research in etiology and identification of sensory and perceptual problems is being integrated in remedial educational approaches. Likewise, parents of autistic children and professionals working with such children are integrating their efforts to create a unified program for those children. Legislation is supporting the development of special programs, and finally it appears that cooperation of various groups and sharing of ideas is becoming more important than conflicts between various ideas or positions.

Thus, there is every hope and indication that the study of autism will progress much more rapidly in the future than it ever has in the past.

BIBLIOGRAPHY

Abeson, A., and Zettel, J. "The End of the Quiet Revolution: The Education for All Handicapped Children Act of 1975." *Exceptional Children* 44(2)(1977):114-30.

Albee, G. W. *Mental Health Manpower Trends: A Report to the Staff Director Jack Ewalt.* New York: Basic Books, 1959.

Bachrach, A. W.; Mosley, A. R.; Swindle, F. L.; and Wood, M. M. *Developmental Therapy for Young Children with Autistic Characteristics.* Baltimore: University Park Press, 1978.

Barsch, R. H. *A Movigenic Curriculum.* Madison, Wisc.: Bureau for Handicapped Children, 1968.

Bartak, L., and Rutter, M. "Educational Treatment of Autistic Children." In *Infantile Autism: Concepts, Characteristics, and Treatment,* edited by M. Rutter. Edinburgh: Churchill and Livingston, 1971.

Bartak, L., and Rutter, M. "Special Education Treatment of Autistic Children: A Comparative Study. I—Design of Study and Characteristics of Units." *Journal of Child Psychology and Psychiatry* 14(1973):161-79.

Bartak, L., and Rutter, M. "Differences between Mentally Retarded and Normally Intelligent Autistic Children." *Journal of Autism and Child Schizophrenia* 6(2)(1976):109-20.

Bateman, B. "Learning Disabilities—Yesterday, Today and Tomorrow." *Exceptional Children* 31(1964):167-76.

Bender, L., and Grugett, A. E. "A Study of Certain Epidemiological Problems in a Group of Children with Childhood Schizophrenia." *American Journal of Orthopsychiatry* 26(1956):131-45.

Bettelheim, B. *A Home for the Heart.* New York: Knopf, 1974.

Bettelheim, B. *The Empty Fortress—Infantile Autism and the Birth of Self.* New York: The Free Press, 1967.

Bristol, M. M. "Continuum of Service Delivery to Preschool Handicapped and Their Families." In *Research to Practice in Mental Retardation,* Vol. 1, edited by P. Muttler. Baltimore: University Park Press, 1977.

Bryson, C. "Short Term Memory and Cross-Modal Information Processing in Autistic Children." *Journal of Learning Disabilities* 5(1972):25–35.

Bryson, C. "Systematic Identification of Perceptual Disabilities in Autistic Children." *Perceptual and Motor Skills* 31(1970):239–46.

Bucher, B., and Lovaas, O. I. "Use of Aversive Stimulation in Behavior Modification." In *Miami Symposium on the Prediction of Behavior, 1967: Aversive Stimulation,* edited by N. R. Jones. Coral Cables, Fa.: University of Miami Press, 1968, pp. 77–145.

Campbell, M. "Biological Intervention in Psychosis of Childhood." *Journal of Autism and Childhood Schizophrenia* 3(4)(1973):367–73.

Campbell, M.; Fish, B.; Korein, J.; Shapiro, T.; Collins, P.; and Koh, C. "Lithium-Chlorpromazine: A Controlled Crossover Study in Hyperactive Severely Disturbed Young Children." *Journal of Autism and Childhood Schizophrenia* 2(1972):234–63.

Campbell, M.; Fish, B.; Shapiro, T.; and Floyd, A. "Imipramine in Preschool Autistic and Schizophrenic Children." *Journal of Autism and Childhood Schizophrenia* 1(3)(1971):267–82.

Cansler, D. P.; Martin, G. H.; and Valand, M. C. *Working with Families.* Winston-Salem, N.C.: Kaplan Press, 1975.

Cantwell, D. P.; Baker, K.; and Rutter, M. "Families of Autistic and Dysphasic Children. Mothers' Speech to the Children." *Journal of Autism and Childhood Schizophrenia* 7(1977):313–27.

Carr, J. "The Severely Retarded Autistic Child." In *Early Childhood Autism,* edited by L. Wing. Oxford: Pergamon, 1976, pp. 247–70.

Casey, La Diane. "Development of Communicative Behavior in Autistic Children: A Parent Program Using Manual Signs." *Journal of Autism and Childhood Schizophrenia* 8(1978):45–59.

Champlin, J. L. "The Efficacy of Home Settings in the Language Training of Low-Functioning Echoic Children." Unpublished doctoral thesis. Nashville, Tenn.: George Peabody College for Teachers, 1970.

Chess, S. "Autism in Children with Congenital Rubella." *Journal of Autism and Childhood Schizophrenia* 1(1)(1971):33–48.

Colman, M. *The Autistic Syndromes.* Amsterdam: North Holland, 1976.

Copobianco, R. J., and Knox, S. "IQ Estimates and the Index of Marital Integration." *American Journal of Mental Deficiency* 68(1964):718–21.

Cox, A.; Rutter, M.; Newman, S.; and Bartak, L. "A Comparative Study of Infantile Autism and Specific Developmental Receptive Language Disorder. II—Parental Characteristics." *British Journal of Psychiatry* 126(1975):146–59.

Creak, M. "Schizophrenic Syndrome in Childhood: Further Progress Report of a Working Party." *Developmental Medicine and Child Neurology* 6(1964): 530–35.

Creak, M., and Ini, S. "Families of Psychotic Children." *Journal of Child Psychology and Psychiatry* 1(1960):156–75.

Creedon, M. P. "Language Development in Non Verbal Autistic Children Using a Simultaneous Communication System." Paper presented at the meeting of the Society for Research in Child Development, Philadelphia. March 1973.

Cruickshank, W. M. *Learning Disabilities in Home, School and Community.* Syracuse: Syracuse University Press, 1977.

Cruickshank, W. M.; Bentzen, F. A.; Ratzburg, F. H.; and Tannhauser, M. T. *A Teaching Method for Brain-Injured and Hyperactive Children.* Syracuse: Syracuse University Press, 1961.

Cruickshank, W. M., and Paul, J. L. "The Psychological Characteristics of Learning Disabled Children." In *Psychology of Exceptional Children and Youth,* edited by W. M. Cruickshank. Englewood Cliffs, N.J.: Prentice-Hall, 1977.

DeMyer, M. "Perceptual Limitations in Autistic Children and Their Relation to Social and Intellectual Deficits." In *Infantile Autism: Concepts, Characteristics, and Treatment,* edited by M. Rutter. London: Churchill and Livingston, 1971.

DeMyer, M.; Churchill, D.; Pontius, W.; and Gilkey, K. "A Comparison of Five Demographic Symptoms for Childhood Schizophrenia and Infantile Autism." *Journal of Autism and Childhood Schizophrenia* 1(1971):175–89.

DeMyer, M.; Norton, J.; and Barton, S. "Social Adaptive Behaviors of Autistic Children as Measured in a Structural Psychiatric Interview." In *Infantile*

Autism: Proceedings of the Indiana University Colloquium, edited by D. W. Churchill *et al.* Springfield, Ill.: Thomas, 1971.

DeMyer, M.; Pontius, W.; Norton, J.; Barton, S.; Allen, J.; and Steele, R. "Parental Practices and Innate Activity in Autistic and Brain-Damaged Infants." *Journal of Autism and Childhood Schizophrenia* 2(1972):49–66.

Desmond, M. M.; Wilson, G. S.; Verniaud, W. M.; Melnick, J. L.; and Rawls, W. E. "The Early Growth and Development of Infants with Congenital Rubella." *Advances in Teratology* 4(1970):39–65.

Fassler, J., and Bryant, N. *Task Performance, Attention and Classroom Behavior of Seriously Disturbed, Communication-impaired, "Autistic"-type Children under Conditions of Reduced Auditory Input.* New York: Columbia University, Research and Demonstration Center, 1970.

Flaharty, R. "EPEC: Evaluation and Prescription for Exceptional Children." In *Autism,* edited by E. R. Ritvo. New York: Halsted, 1976.

Fraser C., and Roberts, N. "Mothers' Speech to Children of Four Different Ages." *Journal of Psycholinguistic Research* 4(1975):9–16.

Gallagher, J. J. *The Tutoring of Brain Injured Mentally Retarded Children: An Experimental Study.* Springfield, Ill.: Thomas, 1960.

Gallagher, J. J., and Wiegerink, R. "Educational Strategies for the Autistic Child." *Journal of Autism and Childhood Schizophrenia* 6(1)(1976):15–26.

Gardner, W. "Use of Behavior Therapy with the Mentally Retarded." In *Psychiatric Approaches to Mental Retardation,* edited by F. J. Menolascino. New York: Basic Books, 1970, pp. 250–75.

Getman, G. N., and Kane, E. R. *Developing Learning Readiness.* New York: McGraw-Hill, 1968.

Goodwin, M. S., and Goodwin, T. C. "In a Dark Mirror." *Mental Hygiene* 53(1969):550–63.

Graham, V. L.; Flaharty, R.; and Richey, E. "Educational Approach at the NPI School." In *Autism: Diagnosis, Current Research and Management,* edited by E. R. Ritvo. New York: Halsted, 1976.

Grossman, F. K. *Brothers and Sisters of Retarded Children: An Exploratory Study.* Syracuse: Syracuse University Press, 1972.

Hamilton, J., and Allen, P. "Ward Programming For Severely Retarded Institutionalized Residents." *Mental Retardation* 5(1967):22–24.

Hazloff, M. A. *Reaching the Autistic Child: A Parent Training Program.* Champaign, Ill.: Research Press, 1973.

Hensley, R.; Hawlin, P.; Berger, M.; Harson, L.; Holbrook, D.; Rutter, M.; and Yule, W. "Treating Autistic Children in a Family Context." In *Autism: A Review of Concepts and Treatment,* edited by M. Rutter and E. Schopler. New York: Plenum, 1978.

Hermelin, B. "Coding and the Sense Modalities." In *Early Childhood Autism,* edited by L. Wing. New York: Pergamon, 1976.

Hermelin, B., and O'Connor, N. *Psychological Experiments with Autistic Children.* Oxford: Pergamon, 1970.

Hewett, F. M. *The Emotionally Disturbed Child in the Classroom.* Boston: Allyn and Bacon, 1968.

Hewitt, F. "Teaching Speech to an Autistic Child through Operant Conditioning." *American Journal of Orthopsychiatry* 35(1965):927–36.

Hobbs, N. *Issues in the Classification of Children.* San Francisco, Calif. Jossey-Bass, 1975.

Hollingshead, A. B., and Redlich, F. C. *Social Class and Mental Illness: A Community Study.* New York: Wiley, 1958.

Holrayd, J. "The Questionnaire on Resources and Stress: An Instrument to Measure Family Response to a Handicapped Member." *Journal of Community Psychology* 2(1974):92–94.

Holrayd, J.; Brown, N.; Wekler, L.; and Simmons, J. "Stress in Families of Institutionalized and Noninstitutionalized Autistic Children." *Journal of Community Psychology* 3(1975):26–31.

Holrayd, J., and McArthur, D. "Mental Retardation and Stress on the Parents: A Contrast Between Down's Syndrome and Childhood Autism." *American Journal of Mental Deficiency* 80(1976):431–36.

Howlin, P.; Mordant, R.; Rutter, M.; Berger, M.; Herrov, L.; and Yule, W. "A Home-Based Approach To The Treatment of Autistic Children." *Journal of Autism and Childhood Schizophrenia* 3(1973):308–37.

Israel, M. "Educational Approaches at the Behavior Research Institute, Providence, Rhode Island." In *Autism: Diagnosis, Current Research and Management,* edited by E. R. Ritvo. New York: Halsted, 1976.

Jones, F.; Simmons, J.; and Frankel, F. "An Extinction Procedure for Eliminating Self-Destructive Behavior in a 9-Year-Old Autistic Girl." *Journal of Autism and Childhood Schizophrenia* 4(3)(1974):241–51.

Kanner, L. "Autistic Disturbance of Affective Contact." *Nervous Child* 2(1943): 217–50.

Kanner, L. "Early Infantile Autism Revisited." In *Childhood Psychosis: Initial Studies and New Insights,* edited by L. Kanner. New York: Wiley, 1973.

Kanner, L. "The Children Haven't Read Those Books." *Actor Paedopsychiatrica* 36(1969):2–11.

Kanner, L. "Problems of Nosology and Psychodynamics in Early Infantile Autism." *American Journal of Orthopsychiatry* 19(1949):416–26.

Kanner, L. *Child Psychiatry.* Springfield, Ill.: Thomas, 1957.

Kanner, L. "Social Adaptation of Autistic Children." In *Childhood Psychosis: Initial Studies and New Insights,* edited by L. Kanner. New York: Wiley, 1973.

Kanner, L., and Lesser, L. "Early Infantile Autism." *Pediatric Clinics of North America* 5(1958):711.

Kephart, N. C. *The Slow Learner in the Classroom.* Columbus, Ohio: Merrill, 1971.

Kirk, S. A., and Bateman, B. "Diagnosis and Remediation of Learning Disabilities. *Exceptional Children* 29(1962):72.

Kirk, S. A., and Kirk, W. D. *Psycholinguistic Learning Disabilities: Diagnosis and Remediation.* Urbana: University of Illinois Press, 1971.

Koegel, R. L., and Rincover, A. "Some Detrimental Effects of Using Extra Stimuli to Guide Learning in Normal and Autistic Children." *Journal of Abnormal Child Psychology* 4(1976):59–71.

Koegel, R. L.; Russo, D. C.; and Rincover, A. "Assessing and Training Teachers in the Generalized Use of Behavior Modification with Autistic Children." *Journal of Applied Behavior Analysis* 10(1977):197–205.

Kozloff, M. A. *Reaching the Autistic Child: A Parent Training Program.* Champaign, Ill.: Research Press, 1973.

Lickstein, K., and Schreibman, L. "Employing Electric Shock with Autistic Children: A Review of the Side Effects." *Journal of Autism and Childhood Schizophrenia* 6(2)(1976):163–75.

Lotter, V. "Epidemiology of Autistic Conditions in Young Children. I—Prevalence." *Social Psychiatry* 1(1966):124-37.

Lotter, V. "Epidemiology of Autistic Conditions in Young Children. II—Some Characteristics of the Parents and Children." *Social Psychiatry* 1(1967):163.

Lovaas, O. I. *The Autistic Child, Language Development through Behavior Modification.* New York: Irvington, 1977.

Lovaas, O. I.; Berberick, B.; Perloff, B.; and Schaeffer, B. "Acquisition of Imitative Speech by Schizophrenic Children." *Science* (1966):705-707.

Lovaas, O. I.; Koegel, R.; Simmons, J. Q.; and Long, J. S. "Some Generalization and Follow-up Measures on Autistic Children in Behavior Therapy." *Journal of Applied Behavior Analysis* 6(1973):131-65.

Lovaas, O. I.; Schaeffer, B.; and Simmons, J. Q. "Experimental Studies in Childhood Schizophrenia: Building Social Behavior by Use of Electric Shock." *Journal of Experimental Studies in Personality* 1(1965):99-109.

Luria, A. R. *The Working Brain, An Introduction to Neuropsychology.* New York: Basic Books, 1973.

MacCulloch, M. J., and Williams, C. "On the Nature of Infantile Autism." *Acta Psychiatrica Scandinavia* 47(1971):295-314.

McNeil, T. F., and Wiegerink, R. "Behavioral Patterns in Pregnancy and Birth: Complications, Histories in Psychologically Disturbed Children." *Journal of Nervous and Mental Disease* 152(5)(1971):315-23.

Miller, A., and Miller, E. "Cognitive Development Training with Elevated Boards and Sign Language." *Journal of Autism and Childhood Schizophrenia* 3(1973):65-85.

Miller, R. "Childhood Schizophrenia: A Review of Selected Literature." *International Journal of Mental Health* 3(1)(1974):3-46.

Morse, W. C.; Cutler, R. L.; and Fink, A. H. *Public School Classes for the Emotionally Handicapped: A Research Analysis.* Washington, D.C.: Council for Exceptional Children, 1964.

Myklebust, H. R. "Learning Disorders: Psychoneurological Disturbances in Childhood." *Rehabilitation Literature* 25(1964):354-60.

National Society for Autistic Children. *On Growing—Up And Away.* Position paper of the NSAC, June 1974, 169 Tampa Ave., Albany, N.Y.

Needels, F., and Jaison, C. "Educational Approaches at the Los Angeles County Autism Project." In *Autism: Diagnosis, Current Research, and Management,* edited by E. R. Ritvo. New York: Spectrum, 1976.

Newsom, C. D. "The Role of Sensory Reinforcement in Self-Stimulatory Behavior." Unpublished doctoral thesis. UCLA, 1974.

Ney, P.; Palvesky, A.; and Markeley, J. "Relative Effectiveness of Operant Conditioning and Play Therapy in Childhood Schizophrenia." *Journal of Autism and Childhood Schizophrenia* 1(3)(1971):337–49.

O'Dell, S. L.; Blackwell, L. J.; Larcen, S. W.; and Hogan, J. L. "Competency-Based Training for Severely Behaviorally Handicapped Children and Their Parents." *Journal of Autism and Child Schizophrenia* 7(1977):231–43.

Ora, J. "Involvement and Training of Parents- and Citizen-Workers in Early Education for the Handicapped." In *Not All Little Wagons Are Red,* edited by M. Karnes. Washington, D.C.: Council for Exceptional Children, 1973.

Ornitz, E., and Ritvo, E. R. "Perceptual Inconstancy in Early Infantile Autism." *Archives of General Psychiatry* 18(1968):76–98.

Ornitz, E., and Ritvo, E. R. "Neurophysiological Mechanisms Underlaying Perceptual Inconstancy in Autistic and Schizophrenic Children." *Archives of General Psychiatry* 19(1968):22–27.

Paluszny, M. "Psychoactive Drugs in the Treatment of Learning Disabilities." In *Learning Disabilities in Home, School, and Community.* Syracuse: Syracuse University Press, 1977.

Pappanikou, A. J., and Paul, J. L., eds. *Mainstreaming Emotionally Disturbed Children.* Syracuse: Syracuse University Press, 1977.

Paul, J. L.; Neufeld, G. R.; and Pelosi, J., eds. *Child Advocacy within the System.* Syracuse: Syracuse University Press, 1977.

Paul, J. L.; Stedman, D. J.; and Neufeld, G. R., eds. *Deinstitutionalization: Program and Policy Development.* Syracuse: Syracuse University Press, 1977.

Paul, J. L.; Turnbull, A.; and Cruickshank, W. M. *Mainstreaming: A Practical Guide.* Syracuse: Syracuse University Press, 1977.

Pauling, L. "Orthomolecular Psychiatry." In *Orthomolecular Psychiatry: Treatment of Schizophrenia,* edited by D. Hawkins and L. Pauling. San Francisco: Freeman, 1973.

Pelosi, J., and Hocutt, A. *The Education for All Handicapped Children Act: Issues and Implications.* Chapel Hill, N.C.: DD Themes and Issues, #10, 1977.

Pribram, K. "Autism: Deficiency in Context-Dependent Processes?" *Proceedings of the National Society for Autistic Children.* Rockville, Md.: Public Health Service, U.S. Department of HEW, 1970.

Polan, C., and Spencer, B. "Checklist of Symptoms of Autism in Early Life." *West Virginia Medical Journal* 55(1959):198-204.

Public Law 93-112. *Vocational Rehabilitation Act of 1973,* Section 504, July 26, 1973.

Public Law 94-103. *The Developmentally Disabled Services and Construction Act of 1975.*

Rappaport, S. R. *Childhood Aphasia and Brain Damage: A Definition.* Narberth, Pa.: Livingston, 1964.

Reichler, R. J., and Schopler, E. "Developmental Therapy: A Program Model for Providing Individualized Services in the Community." In *Psychopathology and Child Development,* edited by E. Schopler and R. J. Reichler. New York: Plenum, 1976.

Reiser, D. "Psychosis in Infancy and Early Childhood, As Manifested by Children with Atypical Development." *New England Journal of Medicine* 15 (1963):269.

Rhodes, W. C., and Head, S. *A Study of Child Variance. Volume III: Service Delivery Systems.* Ann Arbor, Mich.: University of Michigan Press, 1974.

Rhodes, W. C., and Paul. J. L. *Emotionally Disturbed and Deviant Children.* Englewood Cliffs, N.J.: Prentice-Hall, 1978.

Rhodes, W. C., and Tracy, M. *A Study of Child Variance, Volume I.* Ann Arbor, Mich.: University of Michigan Press, 1973.

Rimland, B. "The Differentiation of Childhood Psychoses: An Analysis of Checklists for 2,218 Psychotic Children." *Journal of Autism and Child Schizophrenia* 1(2)(1974):161-74.

Rimland, B. *Infantile Autism.* New York: Appleton-Century-Crofts, 1964.

Rimland, B.; Callaway, E.; and Dreyfus, P. "The Effect of High Doses of Vitamin B_6 on Autistic Children: A Double Blind Crossover Study." *American Journal of Psychiatry* 135(4)(1978):472-75.

Rincover, A. "Sensory Extinction: A Procedure for Eliminating Self-Stimulatory Behavior in Developmentally Disabled Children." *Journal of Abnormal Child Psychology* 6(3)(1978):299–310.

Rincover, A. "Variables in Stimulus-Fading Influencing Discrimination Learning in Autistic Children." *Journal of Abnormal Psychology* (in press).

Rincover, A., and Koegel, R. L. "Setting Generality and Stimulus Control in Autistic Children." *Journal of Applied Behavior Analysis* 3(1975):235–46.

Rincover, A.; Koegel, R. L.; and Russo, D. C. "Some Recent Behavioral Research on the Education of Autistic Children." *Journal of Autism and Childhood Schizophrenia,* in press.

Rincover, A. L.; Newson, C. D.; Lovaas, O. I.; and Koegel, R. L. "Some Motivational Properties of Sensory Stimulation in Psychotic Children." *Journal of Experimental Child Psychology* 24(1977):312–23.

Risley, T., and Wolf, M. M. "Establishing Functional Speech in Echolalic Children." *Behavior Research and Therapy* 5(1967):73–88.

Ritvo, E. R. *Autism: Diagnosis, Current Research and Management.* New York: Halsted Press, 1976.

Ritvo, E.; Cantwell, D.; Johnson, E.; Clements, M.; Benbrook, F.; Slagle, S.; Kelly, P.; and Ritz, M. "Social Class Factors in Autism." *Journal of Autism and Childhood Schizophrenia* 1(3)(1971):297.

Ritvo, E.; Yuiviler, A.; Geller, E.; Kales, A.; Roshkis, S.; Schicor, A.; Plotkin, S.; Axebrod, R.; Howard; and Howard, C. "Effects of L-dopa in Autism." *Journal of Autism and Childhood Schizophrenia* 1(2)(1971):190–205.

Rosenberg, S. A. "Family and Parent Variables Affecting Outcomes of a Parent Mediated Intervention." Unpublished doctoral thesis. Nashville, Tenn.: George Peabody College for Teachers, 1977.

Rubin, E. Z.; Simson, C. R.; and Betwee, M. C. *Emotionally Handicapped Children and the Elementary School.* Detroit: Wayne State University Press, 1968.

Rutter, M. "Autistic Children: Infancy to Adulthood." *Seminars in Psychiatry* 2(1970):435.

Rutter, M. "Childhood Schizophrenia Reconsidered." *Journal of Autism and Childhood Schizophrenia* 2(4)(1972):315.

Rutter, M. "Concepts of Autism: A Review of Research." *Journal of Child Psychology and Psychiatry* 9(1968):1–25.

Rutter, M. "The Development of Infantile Autism." *Psychological Medicine*

4(1974):147–63. [Also reprinted in *Annual Progress in Child Psychiatry and Child Development Education.* Springfield, Ill.: Thomas, 1975, pp. 327–56.]

Rutter, M. "Psychotic Disorders in Early Childhood." In *Recent Developments in Schizophrenia: A Symposium. British Journal of Psychiatry,* edited by Coppen and Walk. (Special publication) 1(1967):133–58.

Rutter, M., and Bartak, L. "Special Education Treatment of Autistic Children: A Comparative Study. II—Follow-up Study and Implication for Services." *Journal of Child Psychology and Psychiatry* 14(1973):241–70.

Rutter, M.; Bartak, L.; and Newman, S. "Autism: A Central Disorder of Cognition and Language?" In *Infantile Autism: Concepts, Characteristics and Treatment,* edited by M. Rutter. London: Churchill and Livingston, 1971.

Rutter, M.; Greenfeld, D.; and Lockyer, L. "A Five- to Fifteen-Year Follow-Up Study of Infantile Psychosis." *British Journal of Psychiatry* 113(1967): 1169–99.

Rutter, M., and Sussenwein, F. "A Developmental and Behavioral Approach to the Treatment of Preschool Autistic Children." *Journal of Autism and Childhood Schizophrenia* 1(1971):376–97.

Salvin, A.; Routh, D. K.; Foster, R. E.; and Lovejoy, K. M. "Acquisition of Modified American Sign Language by a Mute Autistic Child." *Journal of Autism and Childhood Schizophrenia* 7(1977):359–73.

Sameroff, A. J., and Chandler, M. J. "Reproductive Risk and the Continuum of Caretaking Casualty." In *Review of Child Developmental Research 4,* edited by T. D. Harowitz *et al.* Chicago: University of Chicago Press, 1975, pp. 187–244.

Sarason, S., and Gladwin, T. *Psychological Problems in Mental Deficiency.* New York: Harper & Row, 1959.

Schopler, E. "Current Approaches to the Autistic Child." *Pediatric Annals* (March 1973):1–6.

Schopler, E. "Limits of Methodological Differences between Family Studies." In *Autism: A Review of Concepts and Treatment,* edited by M. Rutter and E. Schopler. New York: Plenum, 1978.

Schopler, E.; Brehm, S. S.; Kinsbourne, M.; and Reichler, R. J. "Effect of Treatment Structure on Development in Autistic Children." *Archives of General Psychiatry* 24(1971):415–21.

Schopler, E., and Reichler, R. J. "Parents as Cotherapists in the Treatment of Psychotic Children." *Journal of Autism and Childhood Schizophrenia* 1(1971):87–102.

Schopler, E., and Reichler, R. "Developmental Therapy by Parents with Their Own Autistic Child." In *Infantile Autism: Concepts, Characteristics, and Treatment,* edited by M. Rutter. London: Churchill and Livingston, 1971a.

Schopler, E., and Reichler, R. J. "How Well Do Parents Understand Their Own Psychotic Child?" *Journal of Autism and Childhood Schizophrenia* 2(4) (1972):387–400.

Schopler, E., and Reichler, R. J., eds. *Psychopathology and Child Development: Research and Treatment.* New York: Plenum, 1976.

Skinner, B. F. *Verbal Behavior.* New York: Appleton-Century-Crofts, 1957.

Strain, P. S.; Timm, M. A.; and Wiegerink, R. "New Directions in Research in Preschool Social Behavior: Implications for Teachers." Symposium accepted for presentation at the Annual Meeting of the Council for Exceptional Children, New York. April 1974.

Strain, P. S., and Wiegerink, R. "The Social Play of Two Behaviorally Disordered Preschool Children During Four Activities: A Multiple Baseline Study." *Journal of Abnormal Child Psychology* 3(1)(1975):61–96.

Strain, P. S., and Wiegerink, R. "The Effects of Socio-Dramatic Activities on Social Interaction among Behaviorally Disordered Preschool Children." *Journal of Special Education* 10(1)(1976):71–75.

Strauss, A. A., and Lehtinen, L. *Psychopathology and Education of the Brain-Injured Child.* New York: Grune & Stratton, 1947.

Tanguay, P. E. "Clinical and Electrophysiological Research." In *Autism: Diagnosis, Current Research, and Management,* edited by E. Ritvo. New York: Spectrum, 1976.

Tavormina, J. B.; Ball, N. J.; Dunn, R. L.; Luscomb, B.; and Taylor, J. R. "Psychosocial Effects of Raising a Physically Handicapped Child on Parents." Unpublished manuscript. University of Virginia, 1977.

Tavormina, J. B., and Walker, J. "Evaluation of Respite Care." Unpublished manuscript. University of Virginia, 1976.

Taylor, J. "An Approach to Teaching Cognitive Skills Underlying Language Development." In *Early Childhood Autism,* edited by L. Wing. New York: Pergamon, 1976.

Tompkins, J. Preface. In *Conflict in the Classroom,* edited by N. J. Long, *et al.* Belmont, Calif.: Wadsworth, 1971.

Torrey, E. F.; McCabe, K.; and Hersh, S. P. "Early Childhood Psychosis and Bleeding During Pregnancy." *Journal of Autism and Childhood Schizophrenia* 5(1975):287.

Treffert, D. A. "Epidemiology of Infantile Autism." *Archives of General Psychiatry* 22(1970):431-38.

Turnbull, H. R. III. "The Past and Future Impact of Court Decisions in Special Education." *Phi Delta Kappan* 59(8)(April 1978).

Tustin, F. *Autism and Childhood Psychosis.* New York: Aronson, 1973.

Ward, A. *Childhood Autism and Structural Therapy.* Chicago: Nelson Hall, 1976.

Wiegerink, R., and Mort, K. A. "Teaching Reading to Autistic Children with Use of a Typewriter." Unpublished report. Nashville, Tenn.: George Peabody College for Teachers. 1970.

Wiegerink, R., and Parrish, V. "A Parent-Implemented Preschool Program." *Training Parents to Teach.* First Chance for Children. Technical Assistance Development System. University of North Carolina at Chapel Hill, N.C., 1977.

Wing, L. *Autistic Children: A Guide for Parents.* New York: Brunner/Mazel, 1972.

Wing, L. "Epidemiology and Theories of Etiology." In *Early Childhood Autism,* edited by L. Wing. New York: Pergamon, 1976.

Wing, L., ed. *Early Childhood Autism.* New York: Pergamon, 1976.

Wood, M. M., ed. *Developmental Therapy.* Maryland: University Park Press, 1975.

Wolfensberger, W. *The Principle of Normalization in Human Services.* Toronto: National Institute on Mental Retardation, 1972.

INDEX

Abilities, special: fine motor, 2; memory, 2, 11, 22; musical, 11; premature development, 11
Activity centers, adult, 153
Adults, autistic: need for programs, 143; living arrangements for, 157; vocational program for, 153–57
Advocacy, 101–104, 109
Aggression: drug therapy for, 75; use of inpatient therapy in response to, 86–87; see also Tantrums, Symptoms, self-abuse
Aloneness, preference for. See Symptoms, interpersonal relationships
Anticipatory posture when being picked up, lack of. See Symptoms
Antidepressants. See Drugs
Aphasia, differentiation from autism. See Diagnosis
Audiology: involvement in diagnosis of autism, 28–30
Autism: alternative names for, 1; description of syndrome, 1–3; controversies concerning, 2–3; definitions of, 2–3; first use of term, 3
Autism and Childhood Psychosis (Tustin), 46
Autistic child, case example, 11–15
Autistic Children—A Guide for Parents (Wing), 144
Aveyron, Wild Boy of, 2

Bartak, L.: on education, 120; on etiology, 133; on prognosis, 23; on therapy, 71, 76
Behavior management. See Therapy, behavior modification

Behavior modification. See Therapy, behavior modification
Behavior therapy. See Therapy, behavior modification
Benadryl. See Drugs
Bettelheim, Bruno: on etiology, 46–47, 93–94, 131; on therapy, 70, 131; The Empty Fortress, 46–47
Biochemical therapy. See Therapy, biochemical
Body awareness, program to increase, 121–22
Brain functions: cross-modal associations, 62; figures diagramming, 55–56; general description, 54–59; impairment in autism, 59–68; language, 64–65; memory, 61–62; perceptual problems, 61; see also Cerebral dominance, EEG patterns, Memory, Neurological problems, Perceptual problems, Sensory modalities
Brain injury. See Neurological problems
Brown vs. the Board of Education, 110

Causes of autism. See Etiology
Celiac disease: association with autism, 52–53
Central Nervous System (CNS). See Brain functions, Etiology, organic theories involving CNS impairment
Cerebral dominance, possible lack of in autism, 66
Childhood, normal development in, 6–11
Childhood Autism and Structural Therapy (Ward), 48
Chloral Hydrate. See Drugs

Civil rights of the handicapped, protection of. *See* Laws, P.L. 93–112
Classification of autism, 24–26
Comprehension. *See* Speech and language, receptive language development
Compulsive rituals. *See* Symptoms
Conditioning. *See* Therapy, behavior modification
Cross-modal association defect theory, 62, 116
Cruickshank, William: on interdisciplinary perspective, 99; on learning disabilities, 18, 98; on mainstreaming, 103; on psychoneurological perspective, 99
Curiosity, lack of. *See* Symptoms

Day treatment. *See* Therapy, day treatment
DD law, the. *See* Laws, P.L. 94–103
DDSA (Developmentally Disabled Services and Construction Act). *See* Laws, P.L. 94–103
Deafness, differentiation from autism. *See* Diagnosis and Hearing impairment
Deinstitutionalization, 85, 102–103, 106, 109–10
DeMyer, M., Cross-modal association defect theory, 62; on diagnosis, 22, 100; on etiology, 133–34
Dental services for the autistic, 143–44
Development, normal patterns of, 4–11
Development Therapy Program, 124–25
Developmental disabilities: defined by law, 108–109; inclusion of autism, 25–26, 101, 108–10; state council, 101, 108–10; *see also* Laws, P.L. 94–103
Developmental therapy, 83–84
Developmentally Disabled Services and Construction Act. *See* Laws, P.L. 94–103
Dexedrine. *See* Drugs
Diagnosis: checklists and rating scales, 22–23; controversy surrounding, 1–3; differentiation from brain damage, 37; differentiation from childhood aphasia, 35, 37, 64; differentiation from deafness, 27–29, 37, 43; differentiation from deprivation, 43; dif-

Diagnosis (*cont.*)
ferentiation from elected mutism, 43; differentiation from language delay, 27; differentiation from other conditions and psychoses, 21, 43–44; differentiation from retardation, 21, 24–25, 27, 37, 42–43; differentiation from schizophrenia, 21, 24, 37, 43–44; interdisciplinary perspective, 4, 26–44; *see also* Symptoms
Drug therapy: for aggressive behavior, 75; for epilepsy, 75–76; for withdrawn behavior, 74–75; for sleep disturbance, 76; monitoring of, 74, 76; possible side effects, 73–74; *see also* Drugs
Drugs: antidepressants, negative effects on autistic children, 74–75; Benadryl, used to control sleep disturbances, 76; Chloral Hydrate, used to control sleep disturbances, 76; Dexedrine, negative effects on autistic children, 75; Hormones, used to treat autism, 73–74; Imipramine, negative effects on autistic children, 75; Levodopa (L-dopa), used to treat autism, 72–73; Lithium, used to control self-mutilating behavior, 75; Mellaril, used to control aggression and stereotypic behavior, 75; Phenobarbital, increases aggressiveness, 76; used to control seizures, 76; Prolixin, used to control aggression, 75; Ritalin, negative effects on autistic children, 75; Stelazine, used to control aggression, 75; Stimulants, negative effects on autistic children, 75; Thorazine, used to control aggression, 75; Thyroid, used to treat autism, 73; Tofranil, negative effects on autistic children, 75; Tranquilizers, used to control aggression, 75; Tri-iodothyronine (T_3), used to treat autism, 73; Vitamins, used to treat autism, 72; *see also* Drug therapy

Eating behavior, peculiarities in. *See* Symptoms
Echolalia. *See* Symptoms, communicative speech
Education of emotionally disturbed: ecological perspective, 97–98; historical perspective, 94–97

Education of learning disabled: historical background, 98–100; implications
for autistic, 100–101
Education: effect on prognosis, 17, 133;
goals for autistic child, 130; legal
right of handicapped to, *see* Laws;
programming, 115–30; relation to etiology, 115–60, 130, 158; *see also*
Programs, special
Educational Planning and Placement
Committee (EPPC), 26–27
EEG patterns, abnormal, 49, 54, 66
Electric shock, use in behavior modification, 78–80
Emotional disturbance: autism as, 95;
see also Education of emotionally
disturbed
The Empty Fortress (Bettelheim), 46–47
Environmental theories of autism. *See*
Etiology, environmental theories.
Epidemiology: birth order, 18; incidence, 17; male-female ratio, 17–18,
24; parent characteristics, 18–19, 22,
24, 47–48, 131–32; prevalence, 17;
socioeconomic status, 18, 47
Epilepsy: association with autism, 17,
49, 75–76; drug therapy for, 75–76;
see also Diagnosis
EPPC. *See* Educational Planning and
Placement Committee
Etiology (cause): biogenic theories, *see*
Organic theories; controversies surrounding, 1, 149; environmental theories, problems and evidence against,
45, 47–48, 71, 85, 88, 93–94, 132–34,
152; Bruno Bettelheim, 46–47; Frances Tustin, 46; Leo Kanner, 45–46;
Ward, 48; organic theories involving
CNS impairment, 25, 49, 50–51, 53–
54, 67, 93–94, 132; psychogenic theories, *see* Environmental theories; relation to therapy and education, 115–
16, 130, 158
Eye contact, lack of. *See* Symptoms

Family. *See* Parents, Siblings

German measles. *See* Pregnancy: Ru-
bella during associated with autism
Gingold, parent training program, 136
Group homes, adult, 157

Head Start, required enrollment of the
handicapped. *See* Laws, P.L. 92–
424
Hearing impairment, assessment of in
autistic children, 28–29
Heller's disease, differentiated from
autism, 43
Hermelin, B., central cognitive defect
theory, 61–62, 116
Herpes, during pregnancy, association
with autism, 53–54
Home-based programs of therapy. *See*
Therapy, Home-based programs
Hormones. *See* Drugs
Hospitalization. *See* Therapy, inpatient;
Respite care
Howlin, P., home-based approach, 81,
84–85

IEP. *See* Individualized Education
Plan
Imipramine. *See* Drugs
Incidence of autism, 17
Individualized Education Plan (IEP),
111–12
Infancy: autistic symptoms during, 4–6;
normal development during, 4–6; on-
set of autism in, 1
Inpatient therapy. *See* Therapy, in-
patient
Institute for the Study of Mental Retar-
dation and Related Disabilities
(ISMRRD): interdisciplinary diagno-
sis at, 26–44; dentistry training, 143;
vocational program at, 153–57
Intelligence. *See* IQ
Interdisciplinary perspective: 99, 104,
153–54; diagnosis, 4, 26–44; re-
search, 100; support systems, 103,
137; teaching, 99; training, 105;
treatment, 94
Interpersonal relationships, lack of. *See*
Symptoms
Intonation problems. *See* Symptoms,
communicative speech
Intrapsychic therapy. *See* Therapy, intrapsychic
IQ, 16–17, 23, 25, 49
ISMRRD. *See* Institute for the Study of
Mental Retardation and Related Dis-
abilities

Judevine Center Program, 128–29, 150–51

Kanner, Leo: description of syndrome, 21–23, 34, 131; on classification of autism, 24; on epidemiology, 18, 47; on etiology, 45–46, 131; on prognosis, 16; originator of "autism" as diagnostic category, 2; reported first cases of autism, 2, 149
Koegel, R., on education, 120; on teacher skills, 117
Kozloff, M., on education, 100; on parent training, 134–35; social exchange theory, 81–83

Language. See Speech and language
Language Development Program, 129–30
Laws: effect on autistic, 105–106, 109–10, 112–13; mandatory special education, 26; P.L. 89–313 (money to state institutions for education), 106; P.L. 92–424 (requires enrollment of handicapped in Head Start), 107; P.L. 93–112 (Vocational Rehabilitation Act, protects civil rights of the handicapped), 107–108; P.L. 94–103 (Developmentally Disabled Services and Construction Act), 108–10; P.L. 94–142 (Education for All Handicapped Children Act), 93, 110–13; Title XVIII of the Social Security Act Amendments (Medicare), 106; Title XIX of the Social Security Act Amendments (Medicaid), 106–107
L-dopa. See Drugs
Learning behaviors, influences on: motivation, 118; self-stimulation, reduction of, 119; session structure, 119–20; teacher skills, 117–18
Learning disabilities: 98–100; see also Education of learning disabled
Legislation. See Laws
Levodopa. See Drugs
Lithium. See Drugs
Living arrangements for autistic adults, 157
Lovaas, Ivar: follow-up study on parent training, 132; Language Development

Lovaas, Ivar (cont.)
Program, 81, 123–24, 129–30; on behavior modification with autistic children, 78, 96, 118
Luria, A.: on brain function, 54, 66; on language, 63

McDonald, parent training program, 136
Mainstreaming: 103–104; see also Laws, P.L. 94–142
Medicaid. See Laws, Title XIX of the Social Security Act Amendments
Medical services for the autistic, finding, 143
Medicare. See Laws, Title XVIII of the Social Securities Act Amendments
Megavitamins, 71–72
Mellaril. See Drugs
Memory: problems, 61, 116; special abilities, 2, 11, 22
Metabolic problems, relation to autism, 51–52
Miller, A., and Miller, E., educational approach of, 121–22
Multidisciplinary perspective. See Interdisciplinary perspective

National Society for Autistic Children (NSAC): 142, 146; address of, 142; advocacy efforts of, 101; on deinstitutionalization, 109–10; parents recommend joining, 150
Nature-nurture controversy. See Etiology
Neurological problems: educational programs based on, 115–16; in learning disabilities, 99–100; in retarded autistic, 23; see also EEG patterns, Epilepsy, Etiology, organic theories; Perceptual problems, Sensory modalities
Neurotransmitters: possible involvement in autism, 51–52; see also Seratonin
Non-verbal communication, lack of. See Symptoms
Normalization of environment, 102, 106, 124
NSAC. See National Society for Autistic Children

Operant Conditioning. *See* Therapy, behavior modification
Organic theories of autism. *See* Etiology, organic theories
Ornitz, E., perceptual inconstancy theory, 59–61, 116
Orthomolecular therapy, 71–72
Outpatient therapy. *See* Therapy, outpatient

Pain, lack of reaction to. *See* Symptoms, Stimulation, lack of response to
Parents: acceptance of child's problem, 139–41, 152; affectionate contact with children, 144–45; characteristics of, *see* Epidemiology; evidence against causative role, *see* Etiology; feelings of, 30–32, 140; guidebook for, 144; impact of autistic child on, 146–47; rights under law, 112–13; role of in therapy, 31–32, 81–85, 88, 90–91, 94, 112, 125–47, 152; suggestions from, 150–52; support systems, 30–32, 40, 84, 89, 103, 138–47
Paul, James L.: on advocacy, 101; on education, 97; on learning disabilities, 98–99; on mainstreaming, 103–104
Pauling, Linus, advocate of orthomolecular therapy, 71–72
Pediatrics, involvement in diagnosis of autism, 37–38
Perceptual problems: 59–61, 83–84, 99, 116; *see also* Neurological problems, Sensory modalities
Phenobarbital. *See* Drugs
Play, stereotypic or non-functional. *See* Symptoms, repetitive movements or play
Pregnancy: problems during associated with autism, 4, 41–42, 48, 53–54; rubella during, 4, 49, 53
Prevalence of autism, 17
Prognosis: effect of education on, 17, 133; effect of language ability on, 16, 33; effect of retardation on, 23; factors associated with favorable, 16–17
Programs, special. *See* Development Therapy Program; Judevine Center Program; Language Development

Programs (*cont.*)
Program; Regional Intervention Program; Southeast Mental Health Center Program; Treatment and Education of Autistic and Related Communications Handicapped Children Project; Vocational Programs
Project ReEducation, 95, 105
Prolixin. *See* Drugs
Pronominal reversal. *See* Symptoms, communicative speech
Psychiatry, involvement in diagnosis of autism, 41–44
Psychology, involvement in diagnosis of autism, 39–41
Psychoses, differentiation of autism from other. *See* Diagnosis
Psychosis, autism as a form of, 25–26, 67–68
Public laws. *See* Laws
Punishment. *See* Therapy, behavior modification, negative reinforcement

ReEducation, Project. *See* Project ReEducation
Regional Intervention Project (RIP), 94, 97, 125–26, 137
Reichler, R.: developmental therapy, 81, 83–84; on assessment, 100, 112; on parent training in TEACCH program, 126–27, 134
Reinforcement. *See* Therapy, behavior modification
Repetitive movements. *See* Symptoms
Resistance to change. *See* Symptoms
Respite care: 86, 92, 103, 142–43, 146; for adults, 157; recommended by parents, 150
Retardation: association with autism, 24, 39–40, 87; lowers prognosis for autism, 23; *see also* Diagnosis
Rimland, B.: on diagnosis, 22; on etiology, 51; on megavitamin therapy, 72
Rincover, A.: on behavior modification, 118–19; on education, 120; on teacher skills, 117
RIP. *See* Regional Intervention Project
Ritalin. *See* Drugs
Ritvo, E.: on drug therapy, 72–73; perceptual inconstancy theory, 59–61, 116; on epidemiology, 18; on etiology, 93, 132

Rubella. *See* Pregnancy

Rutland Center. *See* Development Therapy Program

Rutter, Michael: on classification of autism, 24–25; on diagnosis, 23; on education, 100, 120, 130; on epilepsy, 17, 49; on etiology, 48, 133; on language deficit, 62–65; on prognosis, 16–17; on therapy, 71, 76

Sameness, desire for. *See* Symptoms, resistance to change

Schizophrenia, differentiation from autism. *See* Diagnosis

Schopler, E.: developmental therapy, 81, 83–84; on assessment, 100, 112; on education, 120; on etiology, 134; on parent training in TEACCH program, 126–27, 134; on therapy, 131

Self abuse. *See* Symptoms

Self-stimulation. *See* Symptoms

Sensory modalities: cross-modal transfer, 62, 116; development of, 121–22; focus on specific in teaching, 120; relation of self-stimulating behaviors to sensory stimulation, 119; *see also* Symptoms, Stimulation, Perceptual problems

Separation anxiety, lack of. *See* Symptoms

Seratonin: effect of decreasing levels in autistic children, 72–73; levels in autistic children, 52

Services, integration of, 89, 91–92, 104–105

Siblings, effect of autistic child on, 145–46

Sign language, use with autistic, 123, 150

Sleep disturbances, drug therapy for, 76

Social exchange therapy, 82–83, 128

Social relationships. *See* Symptoms, interpersonal relationships

Social smile, lack of. *See* Symptoms

Social work, involvement in diagnosis of autism, 30–32

Southeast Mental Health Center Program, 135–37, 143

Special abilities. *See* Abilities, special

Special education. *See* Education

Speech and language: description of deviant patterns in autism, 33–37; echolalia, *see* Symptoms; communi-

Speech and language (*cont.*)
cative speech, lack of, *see* Symptoms; Lovaas Language Development Program, 129–30; normal development, 5–6, 63–64, 83; pathologist, involvement in diagnosis of autism, 32–37; pronominal reversal, *see* Symptoms; receptive language development (comprehension), 36, 39, 62–65, 122; training to develop, 84, 100, 121–23, 129; vocalization, normal in infancy, 5–6

Stelazine. *See* Drugs

Stereotypic play. *See* Symptoms, repetitive movements or play

Stimulants. *See* Drugs

Stimulation, lack of response to. *See* Symptoms

Stimulation, oversensitivity to. *See* Symptoms

Stranger anxiety, lack of. *See* Symptoms

Symptoms: anticipatory posture when being picked up, lack of, 2, 5, 21; communicative speech, lack of, 1–2, 5–9, 21–23, 32–37, 39, 41, 64, 102, 116, 122; communicative speech, echolalia, 2, 8–9, 21, 23, 34, 122; communicative speech, pronominal reversal, 8, 21, 23, 34, 122; communicative speech, intonation problems, 9–10, 33, 35–36; compulsive rituals, 1, 8, 23, 32; curiosity, lack of, 5; eating behavior, peculiarities, 7–8; eye contact, lack of, 5, 39; interpersonal relationships, lack of, 1–2, 4–6, 8, 21–23, 33, 39, 83, 110; nonverbal communication, lack of, 8, 35–36, 122; repetitive movements or play, 1, 5–6, 9, 23, 118; resistance to change, 1–2, 21, 32; self-abuse, 23, 77–80; self-stimulation, 5, 77, 83, 119; separation anxiety, lack of, 5; social smile, lack of, 4; stimulation, lack of response to, 7, 36, 59–61; stimulation, oversensitivity to, 5, 7, 22, 36, 59–61; stranger anxiety, lack of, 5; three found in all autistic children, 23

Tantrums: if play is interrupted, 6; in reaction to change, 1, 8–9; management of, 31; seemingly unprovoked,

Tantrums (*cont.*)
7, 61; striking out at others in,
10–11; *see also* Aggression
Tavormina, J., on parents' adaptation
to having a handicapped child, 141,
146
Taylor, J., educational approach of,
120–22
TEACCH. *See* Treatment and Education
of Autistic and Related Communications Handicapped Children Project
Teacher skills, 117–18
Tests: hearing, 29; intelligence, 39
"Time out" procedures: recommended
by parents, 151; used in behavior
modification, 78–80
Therapy, behavior modification: 76–81,
84, 88, 90, 115, 117–18; positive reinforcement, 2, 77–78, 80, 82–83, 90,
117–18, 123, 129, 151, 155; educational uses, 96–97, 120–30; parental
use of, 134–35, 137–38
Therapy: biochemical, 71–76; controversies surrounding, 149; day treatment,
90–91; educational methods, *see*
Education; home-based programs,
81–85; ideal model of, 91–92; inpatient, 85–88; intrapsychic, 70–71;
outpatient, 88–90; parents' role in,
see Parents, role in therapy; priorities for, 77, 137–39; relation to etiology, 115–16, 130, 158
Thorazine. *See* Drugs
Thyroid. *See* Drugs
Tofranil. *See* Drugs
Toilet training, problems with, 7
Training programs: for parents, *see* Parents of autistic children, role in therapy; for professionals, 95, 105, 128
Tranquilizers. *See* Drugs
Treatment. *See* Therapy

Treatment and Education of Autistic
and Related Communications Handicapped Children Project (TEACCH),
94, 105, 126–27, 137
Tri-iodothyronine (T$_3$). *See* Drugs
Tustin, Frances: *Autism and Childhood
Psychosis,* 46; on etiology, 46

Uric acid: high levels in autistic children,
52

Violence. *See* Tantrums, Aggression
Visual skills, as step in language devel-
opment, 122
Vitamins. *See* Drugs
Vocalization. *See* Speech and language
Vocational programs, 143, 153–57
Vocational Rehabilitation Act. *See*
Laws, P.L. 93–112

Ward, A.: *Childhood Autism and Structural Therapy,* 48; on etiology, 48;
on therapy, 70–71
Wiegerink, Ronald: on education, 100,
123; on etiology, 132; on parent
training, 125–26, 134
Wing, Lorna: *Autistic Children—A
Guide for Parents,* 144; on incidence
of autism, 17
Withdrawn behavior: drug therapy for,
74–75; *see also* Symptoms, interpersonal relationships, lack of

AUTISM
A Practical Guide for Parents and Professionals

was composed in ten point Compugraphic Times Roman and leaded two points
with display type in Times Roman
by Metricomp Studios, Inc.;
printed on Warren eggshell smooth,
Smyth-sewn, and bound over boards in Columbia Bayside Vellum
by Maple-Vail Book Manufacturing Group, Inc.;
and published by

SYRACUSE UNIVERSITY PRESS
Syracuse, New York 13210